# THREADS OF LACE

## FROM SOURCE TO SINK

### PAT EARNSHAW

GORSE PUBLICATIONS · GUILDFORD

British Library Cataloguing in Publication Data

Earnshaw, Pat

Threads of lace from source to sink
1. Lace, to 1989
1. Title
746.2'.2'.09          ISBN 0-9513891-1-4

Produced by Words & Images, Speldhurst,
Tunbridge Wells, Kent

Printed and bound by Biddles Ltd,
Guildford and Kings Lynn

Typeset by Keyboard Capacity,
Tonbridge, Kent

for Gorse Publications, PO Box 214,
Shamley Green, Guildford GU5 0SW

# THREADS OF LACE
# FROM SOURCE TO SINK

## CONTENTS

ACKNOWLEDGEMENTS

Photographic acknowledgements are given in the individual captions. The following abbreviations have been used for recurring, or longer, names:
B.M.N.H. = British Museum (Natural History)
B.T.T.G. = British Textile Technology Group
V. and A. = Victoria and Albert Museum
W.S.C.A.D. = West Surrey College of Art and Design

Except where otherwise credited, photographs are by the author, or by Ronald Brown.

My gratitude to Rowena Gale, formerly of the Jodrell Laboratories, Kew, for her identification and measurements of the more unusual fibres.

Front cover: the Boramets of Scythia or Tartary, thought at one time to be the source of cotton wool.
Claude Duret, *Histoire admirable des Plantes*, 1605.


Back cover: St. Margaret with a distaff tucked under her arm, the slender spindle apparently supported on the ground. *St. Mary's Psalter*, c1320 (by permission of The British Library).

# 1 Animals, vegetables and minerals make fibres

'Lace is a slender openwork fabric made of *threads*'
(Oxford English Dictionary)

Threads come from a **source**. When they are used, they go into a **sink**, in this instance lace.

The primary sources of threads are plant or animal parts which play a significant, even vital, role in their lives by providing support or protection. A living source is described as organic. Cotton, linen, silk and wool are *organic* threads.

A non-living source is described as *inorganic*. Examples are gold, silver, copper, aluminium and glass. They come from the earth and are minerals. They have no direct connection with living things.

Lurking between organic and inorganic are the fossils, or once-living, now millions of years old and no longer recognizable in the unlikely guises or petroleum and coal. People have resurrected and reissued these fossil substances as artificial or *synthetic* threads: nylon, polyester and acrylic. These people-made, or man-made, fibres provide a third major source of material for the creation of hand and machine laces.

# SOURCES OF THREADS

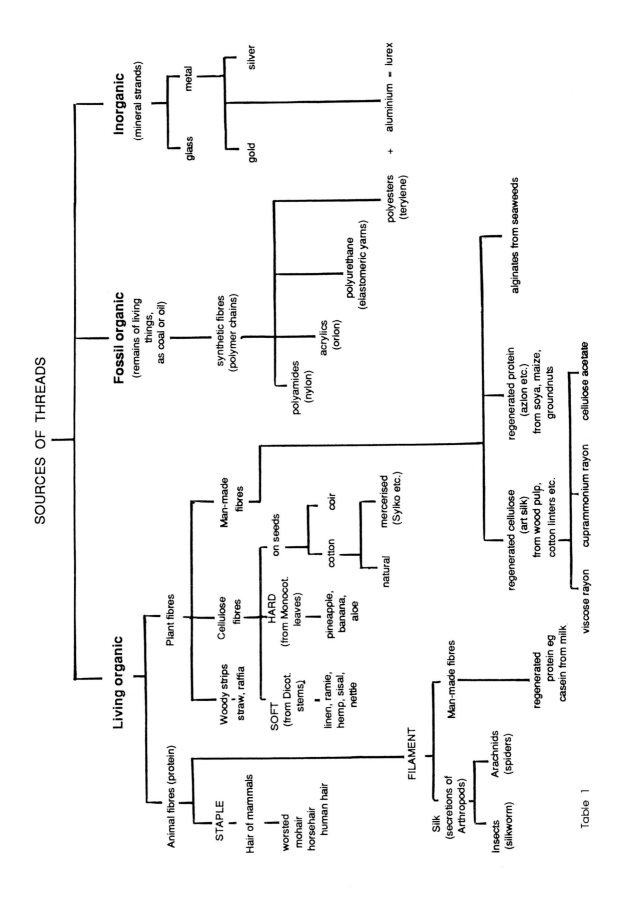

Table 1

# 2 Some dates

The antiquity of the various threads and techniques which were later adapted to the manufacture of lace, is quite staggering. Six thousand years before Christ, wool was being felted for rugs in Turkestan. In northern Europe, a very old textile was recently discovered in mud off the coast of Denmark, and carbon-14 dated to 4200 BC[1]: an early Stone Age period of hunting with as yet no settled agricultural communities. Only a few centimetres in extent, the piece is made of strands extracted from the outer rind of a willow tree twisted into a series of interlocking loops which bear a striking resemblance to the so-called buttonhole stitch destined to become the main structural unit of fashion laces – nearly 6000 years later! (fig. 1).

Early man explored many thread-possibilities; and a whole series of cloth or other fragments made of cow, horse or human hair, pig bristles, sinews, thin strips of animal skin or bark, and fibres pulled from the outer tissues of elm, lime and other trees, have survived. Even more remarkable was the rapid selection of just four main types of thread – linen, cotton, silk and wool – as supremely suitable for fabric-construction. They were derived from totally different sources (see Table 1), were prepared for use in quite different ways, and yet were recognized and utilized throughout almost the whole world, even before history truly began.

Warmer climates cradled the progress of infantile man and, by 13,000 BC, Egypt had attained a level of organization which was not to be reached in north-western Europe until 5000 years later (c 8000 BC). Thus the Ages known as Stone, Bronze and Iron, though they clearly and accurately refer to a level of development, are translated into numerical terms only with difficulty.

### Linen

Tattered pieces of woven linen have survived for 7000 years in Egyptian tombs, but what flash of genius suggested the whole complex rigmarole of

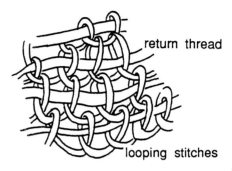

1. Looping (needlebinding) from the Danish Stone Age. This technique, here making a solid fabric, was later used for lace. (after Andersen and Bender Jorgensen).

their construction is beyond imagining. By 2800 BC[2], tomb walls were painted with figures demonstrating various methods of spinning (fig. 2), and it is known that 'royal linens'[3] of that time were of a fine gauze-like texture, their slender threads, made from the green stems of immature flax plants, being so closely woven that there were 200 warps per inch width of fabric. They were highly enough regarded to be reserved for the god-like Pharoah himself.

From this time on, the use of flax plants for textiles spread gradually northwards. By the sixteenth century AD, the plant was cultivated in many areas of western Europe. It was there that lace as a fashion accessory began, and – through over three centuries of prime production – remained. During that whole period, laces were made almost exclusively of linen until, between 1800 and 1900, it was slowly and near-totally replaced by cotton.

The main areas of flax production are Russia, Belgium, France and the Netherlands. England and North America, for whatever reason, never managed to grow good quality flax.

### Cotton

The oldest surviving relics, dating from 3000 BC, were found in the Indus Valley, an area now known as Pakistan. In Peru, grave-cloths woven from cotton have been carbon-dated to 2500 BC. Egypt was later to become very important as a source, but its earliest cultivation and spinning of cotton was probably not before 200–300 AD[4].

Cotton was accepted rather slowly in western Europe, where its vegetable source remained for some centuries an object of myth and mystery. Though it eventually flourished around the Mediterranean, and cottons from the Levant were an important article of trade from the fourteenth century AD, more northerly climates were unsuitable for its growth. From the seventeenth century, as an importation, cotton became increasingly popular in fashion, first as diaphanous muslins, later as lace. Muslin is an Arabic word said to derive from the town of Mosul (Iraq), some 250 miles north of Baghdad and close to the site of the ancient city of Ninevah.

The famous Dacca muslins are referred to as 'calicuts' in the mid-seventeenth century *Travels* of Taverner. They were woven in several places in Bengal, then carried away to a place of large meadows and lemon trees where they were dipped in lemon water and stretched on the grass to whiten. 'Some calicuts are made so fine you can hardly feel them in your hand and the thread when spun is scarcely discernable . . . when a man puts the calicut on his skin he shall appear as plainly as if he was quite naked'. This superb muslin was reserved for the seraglio of the Great Mogul, or his nobles. It was fully appreciated: the women for coolness wore nothing else. Its manufacture was highly specialized and timelessly slow: 'Muslins are made by a few families so exceptionally fine that four months are required to weave one piece which sells at 400 to 500 rupees. When this muslin is laid on the grass and the dew has fallen upon it it is no longer discernable'[5]. A turban which required 35 to 40 yards of such muslin weighed only four ounces (fig. 3).

As for Europe, documentary records prior to the eighteenth century must be treated with caution. The precise anatomical source of cotton was not understood, the plant itself being totally unknown locally. It was assumed by many to be a stem fibre similar to flax. Thus Pepys in 1664, in the early days of muslin importation, records a discussion between a Customs official and the East India Company as to 'whether calicos [muslins] be linnen or no . . . they say it is made of cotton woole, and grows upon trees, not like flax or hemp'[6]. The aim of the debate was to determine the amount of duty that should be paid on it, and the decision went in favour of cotton being a kind of linen, a confusion which persisted for a long time. Even the *Cyclopaedia* of Ephraim Chambers, in 1738, defines cotton as 'a sort of wool or rather flax'. 'Cotton' could also indicate a brushed wool, or even the tow fibres of linen which, being fluffy, made the thread and fabric look cottonized. Hemp, similar in source to linen, was also for many years not distinguished from it by name.

### Silk

The rise of silk began in the Far East, reputedly when Si-Ling, wife of the Emperor Huang-Ti succeeded, in 2640 BC, in domesticating a species of

2. Spinners in Egypt, c2800 BC, Beni Hasan tombs, no. 17. Note the domesticated animals (Newberry).

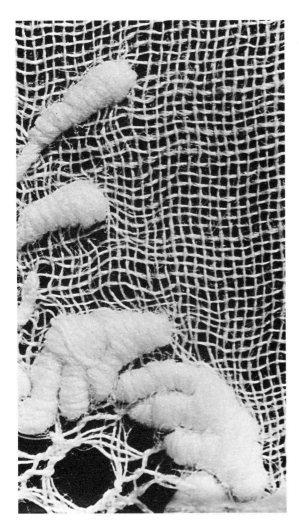

3. Indian cotton muslin, 18th century AD, with embroidery and pulled threadwork. Note the variations in thread thickness, and the looseness of the weave.

silkworm known as *Bombyx mori*, which feeds on the leaves of the white mulberry tree. For 3000 years from that date the monopoly of its production was held by the Imperial dynasties of China. In 300 AD silkworm cultivation spread to Japan, and then the eggs were smuggled to India, and the culture extended gradually westwards, first to Syria and Persia, to Spain and Italy by the eighth century AD and to England and France by the fifteenth. While silk-weaving, using imported yarn, flourished in England from the fourteenth century, attempts at sericulture by James I in the early seventeenth century, and later ventures set up in Ireland in 1825 and again in 1942[7] failed, the climate being unsuitable for the intensive planting of mulberry trees.

However *Bombyx* flourished in the warmer areas of southern Europe, where its preferred food was available in generous quantities.

Silk bobbin laces were being made in Venice and Switzerland in the second quarter of the sixteenth century, and from then on, in their natural shades of pale gold, or dyed black or more vivid colours, they played a secondary role to the ubiquitously dominant linen.

### Wool

This is regarded as the earliest fibre to have been used for textiles. The first references are again from Asia, where advanced civilizations developed while western Europe was still in the grip of barbarians. Babylonia, which flourished in the Euphrates valley from 7000 BC, is said to have meant 'land of wool'. Flocks of sheep and goats were already domesticated during the New Stone (Neolithic) Age, initially for the sake of their meat and skins, and this nomadic activity was well established by the Bronze Age. In Mesopotamia (Iraq) this was before 3000 BC; in northern Europe it began about 1800 BC; while Arizona, Mexico and Peru had advanced no further only a few centuries ago[8]. There were no efficient implements for shearing until the Iron Age, but the downy underfleece or the shaggy outer coats could certainly have been combed or plucked from the animal, living or dead. Shearing of sheep is referred to a number of times during the Exodus of the Israelites from Egypt, *c*1450 BC, and goat's hair was used for the tabernacle curtains[9]. The prehistoric wool felts of Turkoman were made of compressed goats' hair, and sheep's wool was being spun several centuries before Christ, as evidenced by Danish textiles dated at 1500 BC. In Britain, the Romans about 50 BC to 400 AD established a wool factory for blankets and clothing, to protect their occupying armies from the inclement weather, and looms set up in Winchester wove yarns so fine they were said to be 'in a manner comparable to a spider's web'[10]. Britain's wool trade was the mainstay of her economy for centuries until, by 1814, its importance was superseded by cotton.

As far as lacemaking is concerned, although wool was certainly being used in the seventeenth century, and had a brief flash of fashion in the nineteenth, it was never a truly popular thread except for the decoration of peasant costume.

### Man-modified fibres

**Mercerised cotton** Mercerisation, an industrial process named after the inventor, John Mercer, was discovered almost accidentally in 1844 during attempts to find a way of strengthening machine-spun cotton thread which, when very fine, was almost too fragile to be economically viable. The natural cotton was treated with caustic soda. This strengthened but also shrank it. In 1890 shrinkage was stopped by clamping the yarn or fabric in place as it dried and, by 1895, the thread was a commercial success[11]. A side effect of the process was an elimination of the twists and a smoothing out of the wrinkles which marked the natural yarn, producing an uncorrugated surface which reflected light more evenly making the threads appear brighter and almost silk-like. They also dyed more readily.

In the years which followed, the expense of pure silk, and even more importantly its scarcity, following the near-extermination of the worms by the disease pébrine in the mid-nineteenth century, accelerated the search for a silk substitute.

**Man-made fibres** are created by the manipulation of already-existing organic substances. Their source – like that of linen, cotton, silk and wool – is living or once-living organisms. The extent of the alteration, from the original source to the final yarn, has resulted in a commercial distinction between 'man-made' and 'synthetic'.

(a) MAN-MADE fibres are regenerated from complex organic compounds, changed a little but not basically altered from the time when they were inside, or attached to, plants and animals. The first to appear was 'artificial silk' developed in 1884 by Count Hilaire de Chardonnet from cotton unfit for spinning. His yarns looked alright, but the nitrocellulose process which he used had a tendency to explode. A more stable cuprammonium form was discovered in 1890; a viscose form in 1892; and acetate or cellulose acetate in the 1940s. The first two were renamed 'rayon' in 1924[12].

A different form of regenerated fibre, casein, could be made from skimmed milk. Although developed in 1898, it was not commercially successful as a yarn until 1935 when lanital, with similarities to natural wool, was developed in Italy. Maize, soya bean and ground nuts, could also produce 'regenerated protein fibres' but these date only from after the Second World War and have not been used for laces.

(b) SYNTHETIC threads are derived from the fossil fuels coal and petroleum. They are still organic in origin, but their source is plants and animals which died some 30 to 400 million years ago. The chemical breakdown involved in their conversion is very extensive and the fibres no longer bear any resemblance either chemical or physical to their primary source.

The first experiments in this field date from the 1920s and 30s, when non-thread plastics and artificial rubber were being produced. The first actual threads were nylon, developed by the American, Dr Wallace Carothers. They were commercially launched in 1938, opening up an entire new era in textile manufacture[13]. Polyesters followed in 1941 and acrylics in 1944. In each case full commercial production began several years later. A wide range of variants of these threads has developed since that time, many of them used for machine laces.

### Mineral threads

The bronze of the Bronze Age was an alloy of between 67 to 95% copper with zinc, tin, lead or silver. The use of gold for ornament dates back to at least 4000 BC, but for textiles the earliest reference is around 1250 BC. The making of a priestly vestment (ephod) for Aaron – using an inweaving of gold with 'fine twined linen' is described in Exodus (39 vv.2,3): 'and they did beat the gold into thin plates, and cut it into wires and work it in the blue and the purple and the scarlet and in the fine linen, with cunning work'.

In the Middle Ages, gold threads were silver-gilt, i.e. silver wires were plated with gold. However for the solid braids and openwork passements of the sixteenth century, pure gold (24 carat) might well be used. This extravagance came to an end with the excessive influx of precious metals from Peru and Mexico when the Conquistadores, adding to their other destructive activities, brought back such huge quantities to Europe that the currencies of gold and silver coin, then universally in use, were totally devalued. During the seventeenth and eighteenth centuries, copper and silver in varying quantities were mixed with the gold, reducing the carat, changing the colour and increasing the tendency to tarnish. Such transiently glittering threads, giving a false impression of value, were known as tinsel or clinquant. By the end of the nineteenth century, gold wire for lacemaking (mainly for church or carnival purposes) was likely to be pretty far removed from purity, consisting of 90 parts silver, seven of copper, and only 3 of gold for gold-plating[14]. This produced a rather brassy effect, quickly dulled by oxidation.

# 3 *Fibres are chemicals*

So far we have talked rather vaguely of strips, strands and fibres as the stuff of which threads are made. The essence of a thread, particularly in relation to lace, is that it should be very long and thin; flexible without being floppy; strong enough to endure the initial friction of manufacture and the later traumata of wash and wear; with limited elasticity but adequate resilience so that it keeps its shape; a good drape so that it sits or hangs well; a gentle lustre; a neutral colour; a smoothness that does not deteriorate into a halo of fluffiness clouding the design; and, hard to define but no less essential, an aspect of beauty.

This rather demanding catalogue perhaps helps to explain why, of all the millions of plants and animals on the earth, so very few are able to contribute anything useful in the way of threads for lace.

Basically what these exclusively special fibre-producing plants and animals must have are chemicals made up of ultra-large blocks or macro-molecules which lie lengthwise so that they already form in their natural state miniature fibres or fibrils. The blocks are known as *polymers*, and in theory they have only to be stuck together end to end to form a yarn or thread. In practice it is not so simple.

## Cellulose

A polymer [a Greek word, meaning simply 'many parts'] is best visualized as a long chain of similar links which may vary in number from 200 to 10,000. In plants, the chemical nature of the polymer fibril is cellulose, an essential constituent of the walls which enclose and support the living contents of every cell. Cellulose is made of three elements – carbon, hydrogen and oxygen – grouped together in the basic proportions; $C_6 H_{10} O_6$. This unit, already quite large, is bonded to a similar one with the loss of an oxygen. In the cotton polymer, some 2000 of these units are linked together, producing for the entire structure (macromolecule) a weight estimated at between 200,000 and 330,000 (or even 1.600,000) depending mainly on which of the possible methods

of determining its weight has been used (viscosity, ultra-centrifuge, gel permeation chromatography etc). There is a further problem, that any chemical reaction and many physical effects reduce the size of the molecule, so that the very process of weighing it may make it smaller.

Viscose rayon, which is also cellulose, has 250 units or links in its chain; cuprammonium has 500; and cellulose acetate 300.

The linkages are strong, but they can be broken by harmful agents such as acids and light, making the chain shorter, so that it has fewer links or, in technical terms, a lower *degree of polymer-ization*. Thus the chain is weakened, its stability is reduced and it is more easily damaged by antagonistic forces.

The units of the cellulose polymer are really forms of glucose sugar, and this is something to bear in mind when lace threads are damaged or degraded, since sugar dissolves readily in water, and excessively badly treated lace could slowly disintegrate into a syrupy puddle.

The chemistry of lace threads is in fact extremely relevant to their health and stability. Cellulose is broken down by sulphuric acid (resulting from industrial or domestic sulphur dioxide in the air which hydrolyses it); by oxidation (produced by the action of chlorine bleaches for example); by friction (even vibrations in a textile mill can be damaging); by light (which however dim provides energy for oxidation processes); and by moulds which digest the cellulose for food, causing the lace to rot away. In less extreme instances, or stages in this downward path, the extent of the damage can be expressed as a proportional reduction in the degree of polymerization (or DP, sometimes referred to as the degree of viscosity or holding-together-power). In viscose rayon, oxidation during ageing can reduce its molecular weight by half[15]. The lower the DP of a thread, in comparison with its healthy state – say 2000 in cotton – the sicker the polymer, the weaker the thread, and the more fragile, or nearer to falling apart, the lace.

Although linen, cotton and artificial silk are all cellulose, regarded chemically, this does not make them identical. The chemistry of threads is like the foundations of a house, determining its size and shape, but leaving open the possibilities for such a wide variety of structures to be built upon it that a surface examination of them may well fail entirely to spot their basic similarity.

### Proteins

Cellulose is never found in animals, and their fibres derive from quite a different and more complicated chemical: protein. In addition to the elements carbon, hydrogen and oxygen, proteins always contain nitrogen, and sometimes other elements as well. Wool for example contains sulphur.

Like cellulose, the animal proteins used for threads have, in themselves, a fibre-like structure, but here the units are not glucose but amino acids. They too have the ability to line themselves up in a chain-like manner, as if they were indeed preparing to become threads.

In fibroin (silk), there are mainly four different amino acids: glycine, alanine, serine and tyrosine. The elements are arranged in the approximate proportions: $C_{15} H_{23} N_5 O_6$. The molecular weight of the polymer is probably between 50,000 and 300,000[16].

The protein keratin (wool) is not fully extended in a straight line, as silk is. Instead its polymers have a spiral form, reflected in the crinkly nature of the fibres themselves. This gives them an elasticity which enables them to stretch and recoil like tiny springs. Some seventeen different amino acids are involved in their construction, the polymer consisting of some 600 units each with a chemical formula of $C_{42} H_{157} N_5 S O_{15}$. The single S here represents sulphur, contributed by the amino acid cystine. In wool, some of its amino acids are basic and others acidic, giving it a ready affinity for dyes.

### Man-made and synthetic fibres

Any fibres created by man must take on chain-like forms if they are ever to be successful as threads:

*polymers make fibrils make fibres make threads make lace.*

In nylons (polyamides) the relatively simple units are linked by amides, for example hexamethylene diamine is reacted with adipic acid; in terylene (polyesters) the units are linked by ester groups; and in orlon (acrylics) it is acrylonitrile units which are joined together. In effect these substances are taking the place of the glucose units of cellulose, and the amino acid units of proteins. The same DP formula applies: the longer the chain, the greater the number of links and the stronger the fibre. The minimum molecular weight for a usable fibre is 4000, and yarns for commercial purposes need a molecular weight of over 10,000. Nylon 6.6 has an MW of 50,000, and its DP is 205[17].

Synthetic elastics are made of elastomeric yarns. Chemically these are polyurethanes. Some are used for machine laces.

In the regenerated cellulose fibres of artificial silks, and the regenerated proteins derived from skimmed milk, soya bean etc, although the fibres do not come immediately from plants and animals, and although their use may involve quite complex re-organizational techniques, their chemical structure still remains closely similar to that of the natural forms from which they are derived. However, while the cellulose is already in fibril form, the proteins used are of a rounded or globular form, and have to be straightened out in order to be converted into fibres. It is questionable how economically profitable such a procedure is.

Alginate fibres come from brown seaweeds in which alginic acid replaces cellulose as the walls of the cells, and the polymers lie straight and fibre-like, side by side. The product of the manufacturing process is calcium alginate, a compound readily soluble in sodium carbonate and easily washed away with soap when its usefulness as a temporary support during lacemaking is over.

### Minerals

Chemically, silver and gold are minerals which never at any time formed part of a living organism. Their molecular nature is extremely simple: they are not even compounds but elements, represented by the chemical symbols Au (aurum = gold) or Ag (argentum = silver). The somewhat less precious metal, copper (Cu) has also at times played a part in the lacy decoration of garments. Copper wire for example might be plated with gold, silver or nickel, or alloyed with zinc to form brass. These minerals do not have a natural fibre-like form. Any threads created from them begin as solid lumps cut from the earth or dredged from streams, then purified and drawn out into wires or beaten into a thin foil which afterwards is sliced into narrow strands. In short, threads of gold, silver and copper are artificially manufactured by a purely physical rather than a chemical process.

The only other metal appearing in commercial laces is aluminium. This, combined in various ways with synthetics, can produce the artificial thread-metal lurex, for example by sandwiching a thin sheet of aluminium between coatings of polyester or cellulose acetate film, the sandwich then being cut into narrow strips (fig. 4 colour). Alternatively, polyester film can be coated with aluminium which is lacquered to produce brilliant non-tarnishing gold, silver or other metallic tints.

Another mineral, glass, can be strongly heated and drawn out to make hard flexible fibres. It was used experimentally in the nineteenth century and a bobbin lace made at Bedford was exhibited at 'the World's Fair' in 1851. It comprised:

'a union of spun-glass with spun-thread, the ground being made of the ordinary material, but the pattern composed of the finest spun-glass, of a delicate lilac colour. At some distance, this might have been mistaken for floss-silk … The impossibility of submitting this lace to the purifying influence of soap and water, together with the liability of the glass to break on meeting with any but the most tender treatment, must prevent its practical adoption'[18].

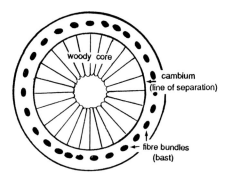

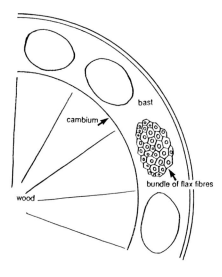

5a.  The main regions of the flax stem, in cross-section.

5b.  Detail of a bundle showing the shape of the cells
(ultimates) in cross-section, and the line of the cambium
where the bast is separated from the wood core during
braking and scutching.

6.  Pulling flax plants by hand, and stacking them for drying
(Trecco).

# 4 The physical nature of fibres

Chemically, fibres fall into a small number of sharply defined categories:

Cellulose polymers
Protein polymers
Regenerated cellulose or regenerated protein polymers
Synthetic or synthesized polymers
Mineral/metal elements.

Fibres differ in their physical as well as in their chemical nature. They differ also in their precise source, that is in the role they played in the plant or animal from which they originated. They differ in appearance, length, width, shape in cross-section, surface features (scales, twists, kinks etc), colour, resistance to breakage (tensile strength), lustre (ability to reflect light), elasticity and water absorption; in their reaction to stains, and to heat; and in their behaviour during drying. All these features can help to determine which thread has been, or should be, used in any particular lace.

The source of vegetable fibres may be from the stems or leaves of flowering plants where they serve for support; or from the seeds where they serve for protection from abrasion, desiccation and saturation, and also at times help with dispersal. Stem fibres are described as soft, and leaf fibres as hard.

Animal fibres can be obtained from the hairy covering of mammals (warm-blooded animals that produce milk); or from the oral secretions of Arthropods (spineless animals with jointed external skeletons).

Short fibres are known as *staples* (linen, cotton, wool) and long fibres as *filaments* (silk, regenerated and synthetic fibres).

### Stems (soft fibres)

Stem fibres come only from that group of plants known as Dictoyledons, which have fairly long stems with broad leaves. Since these so-called soft fibres are concerned with mechanical support, they have a natural strength and resilience enabling the plant to bend without breakage by the wind or other forces, and to spring back again to their original position once the pressure is released. Although they are present in a wide variety of flowering plants, only the fibres of flax are of outstanding importance to lace. However ramie, hemp, nettle and others have at times been used. The quality of the fibres – length, pliability, durability and so on – are obviously of great significance, but the factors which most determine the usage of fibres from any particular plant are primarily economic ones – lace being essentially a commercial production – based on ease of growth, problems of extraction of the fibres, cost of preparation of the thread and, of course, market demand – this latter being not always rationally accounted for.

**Linen**  The fibres for linen thread are obtained from an annual plant, *Linum usitatissimum* (= most useful flax). The plant and its fibres are referred to as flax; the threads made from the fibres, and the lace or other fabrics made from the threads, are referred to as linen.

The fibres are internal, concentrated in a cylindrical area, the *bast*, or inner cells of the bark (fig. 5a). The fibres as used are long, but each is built up of short units or *ultimates*, which in fact are cells, known as sclerenchyma. The fibres are arranged in some fifteen to forty groups or bundles, each bundle containing up to forty individual fibres in cross-section (fig. 5b). The cells are elongated in a vertical direction, and each has a central cavity (lumen) surrounded by walls heavily thickened with cellulose which is composed, as we already know, of chain-like polymers. To the inside of the bast area is a thin circle of growing cells, the cambium. Within that again is the central core of woody tissue where water is carried from the roots to the upper parts of the plant.

The seedling plants are sown close together so that they grow tall, thin and straight, stretching upwards towards the sun. Traditionally, when they are ready, and the stems are still only a few milli-metres in diameter, the plants are pulled up by the roots, tied in 'beets' (fig. 6), and stacked for about fourteen days to dry out. The seeds are then removed by *rippling*, and the fibres rescued from their imprisonment within the stem by *retting*, a rotting process which results in the disintegration of the cambium and other soft cells into a thick, slimy and odoriferous mush, enabling the bast with its long and valuable fibres to be separated, without damage, from both the outer skin and the inner core, and the bundles from each other.

The bacteria or fungi which cause the rotting need moisture for their digestion. This can be provided in a number of ways: by running water such as the Nile in Egypt or the River Lys at Courtrai; by artificial ponds or dams, a method favoured by Mechlin, Bruges and other Flemish centres; or even by repeated exposure to heavy dew. The first is the gentlest process, slowing the greedy outpour of juices which break down the stems, and allowing the fibres to ease away more gently from their surroundings so that they achieve a fine quality and a palely golden hue. Stagnant water favours more rapid breeding of the hungry agents of decay, while the minerals present in the soil around the dams may tint the fibres a light steel-grey – seen perhaps in the Flanders bobbin lace collar and cuffs worn by Henrietta Maria in the 1625 painting by Van Dyck (fig. 7 colour); or an earthy brown from the peat bogs of Ireland or the Netherlands. In dew (ground or field) retting, the destroying organisms are fungi which actually burrow inside the stems and that, as well as the daily alternation of damp and dry, causes a harshness of texture incompatible with good lacemaking.

Retting is a highly skilled procedure since precisely the right moment must be chosen to stop the rot. If the flax is under-retted, the fibres will fail to separate satisfactorily, the residues of the other tissues will cling to them, and they will appear green. If it is over-retted the bundles will break apart too much. Then, in effect, the fibres will shorten until they become usable only for a fluffy weakish thread. The effect of retting on the quality of flax fibres is thus very significant.

Next, the bundles are *broken* by the stems being crushed lengthwise between fluted rollers. *Scutching*, which follows, consists of beating the crushed stems with blunt metal or wooden blades until the wood and other unwanted tissues fall away. *Hackling* completes the work of cleaning the fibres and of removing the shorter ones known as *tow*. The longer

8. Flax fibre cells in cross-section and side view (courtesy: B.T.T.G.).

*line* fibres are combed until they lie parallel to each other like coarse strands of grey or yellowish-white hair. They are still in groups, the individual fibre-cells being lightly stuck together both end to end and side by side. The extent of further separation must be carefully controlled in accordance with the quality of thread required. On no account must the fibres be allowed to separate completely into their ultimates, which may be only half-an-inch long. Only in their full length can they give good linen. Cotton-ization, the deliberate breaking-up of the fibres in order to machine-spin them like the short staples of cotton, proved unsatisfactory, the fragments lacking the pliability and adhesion (ability to cling), possessed by cotton itself.

The structure of the individual fibres is shown in fig. 8. In cross section they are angular, with five or six sides. Their thick walls and narrow central cavi-ties (lumina) are clearly seen, also the way in which they are grouped together. The side view of a single fibre shows characteristic lumps or nodules like mildly arthritic fingers which make the linen threads of lace easy to identify under the microscope. Though this feature appears in other bast fibres such as hemp, only flax is commonly used for laces.

The outermost fibrils of the flax ultimates do not lie entirely straight but in a wide spiral. When they are moistened, the fibrils swell and shorten, rotating the free end in a clockwise (Z) direction (looked at from below). As they dry out again, they twist in an anti-clockwise (S) direction (fig. 9). This physical property, like the nodules, is not unique to flax, but helps to distinguish it from cotton.

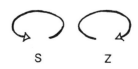

S          Z

9. Spiralling of flax fibres: left, drying; right, absorbing water.

### Leaves (Hard fibres)

Leaf fibres are obtained not from broad-leaved plants, as are bast fibres, but from plants (mostly of the Iris order of Monocotyledons) which have sword-shaped leaves often growing in a group from ground level, the stem itself being subterranean, except in the case of palms and other tropical forms where the tuft of leaves may be raised to a considerable height at the top of a temporary or permanent stalk of trunk-like appearance (fig. 10). In the broader leaves of Dicotyledons, the fibres form a delicately branching network which is useless for thread production. The comparatively narrow leaves of Monocotyledons on the other hand have straight unbranched veins supported by long fibres which are lignified, or woody, making them hard, springy, and too resilient for most lacemaking techniques (fig. 11). Veins and fibres are firmly stuck together, and the task of separating them from the surrounding tissues is more difficult than is the case with bast.

However the fibres of pineapple (*Ananas comosus*), are of exceptional quality, some of them finer than flax, only six microns in diameter[19]. Like the fibres of bast, those of leaves are internal. To prepare them for use, the mature leaves are cut, retted by immersion in fresh water for five to ten days, then taken to a clear running stream and scraped with a piece of broken pottery or a mollusc shell to clean away the softened tissues. The finer fibres are separated out, dried, and passed on to the preparer of yarn. A quicker method is to feed the leaves through the rollers of a machine similar to an old-fashioned wringer or mangle.

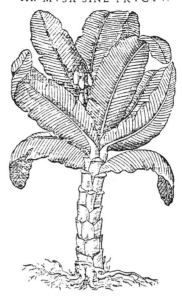

III. MVSA SINE FRVCTV.

10. A typical palm tree, '*Musa* without fruit'. Probably banana. (Dalechamps).

The Banana plant, *Musa sapientium*, produces similar fibres. Its better-known relative, abaca or Manila hemp (*Musa textilis*), was in use in the Philippines in 1521 at the time of Magellan's visit. Pineapple, banana and abaca all grow in tropical or sub-tropical climates where their large leaves can give very long fibres. In theory, temperate Monocotyledons such as Solomon's Seal (fig. 12) could also be used. but their much smaller size would make the work tedious.

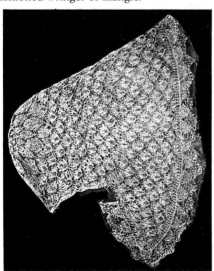

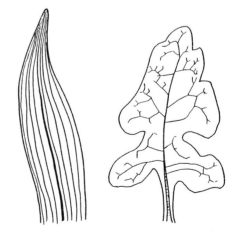

11. The characteristic arrangement of veins and fibres in left, a Monocot.; right, a Dicot., leaf.

12. A knitted cap, c1840, said to be made from the fibres of solomon's seal.

### The coverings of seeds

Although many seeds carry extrusions of hair, only one is of economic importance where textiles and lace are concerned, and that is cotton.

**Cotton** (*Gossypium* species, Mallow family)   Being a native of warm and sub-tropical lands, the cotton plant was unfamiliar to ancient travellers from northern Europe, and prompted strange tales of animal-plants, or zoophytes, observed in Tartary and Samarkand (that broad area stretching from Astrakhan on the Caspian Sea, through central Russia, to Mongolia and northern China) such as Duret's Boramets of 1605 (see front cover), a sheep-like creature raised three feet above the ground on a central stalk and feeding happily on the surrounding vegetation. Duret himself was not entirely gullible. In a long dissertation covering two full pages, he speculates on the creature's true nature attempting, in a world where so much was still unfamiliar, to interpret what he did not know in terms of what he did. He noticed for example that although the Boramets appeared like a sheep, yet carnivores did not attack nor try to eat it. In fact it is a true plant, an ancient type of fern or clubmoss, having a thick underground stem covered with the shaggy remnants of leaf bases which give it a fleece-like appearance. The plant was called in antiquity the Scythian lamb (*Agnus scythians*), for it did resemble a lamb, though one lying on its back with its feet in the air and an additional central stalk like a persistent umbilical cord pointing vertically upwards. It was perhaps natural for travellers to reverse the plant's normal position to rob it of its disquieting mystery. The resultant confusion was compounded by the similarity between the Russian name for the plant, Baranetsù, and that for a sheep, Baranù.

Some writers relied on much earlier records, such as those of Herodotus who visited Scythia (the area to the north of the Black Sea) about 450 BC. On seeing the cotton tree he wrote: 'The wild trees of that country bear fleeces as their fruit, surpassing those of the sheep in beauty and excellence; and the Indians use cloth made from this tree wool'. An even more graphic description, illustrated by an engaging woodcut of a cotton tree with its pods bursting open to release tiny rams (fig. 13), was given by Sir John Mandeville in his *Voiage and Travail*, a fourteenth-century compilation of older stories, possibly going back to the first or second centuries AD to dip into the *Materia Medica* of Dioscorides. This lamb-tree was discovered

'by Cathay [China] towards High India . . . and there groweth a maner of Fruyt, as thoughe it weren Gowrdes: and when thei ben rype, men kutten hem a to, and men fynden with inne a lytylle Best, in Flessche, in Bon and Blode, as though it were a lytylle Lomb, with outen Wolle. And men eten bothe the Frut and the Best: and that is a gret Marveylle. Of that Frute I have eten; alle thoughe [thought?] it were wondirfulle . . .'

The idea of eating a real cotton boll would seem to make nonsense of the analogy, and indeed ambiguity abounds. For example does 'with outen Wolle' mean 'without wool' (lacking wool) or does it mean 'with wool on the outside'? The illustration, and also the phrase 'man fynden with inne' where 'with inne' can only mean 'inside', seem to indicate that the little lambs were indeed covered with a fleece, though it is hard to see then how they could tempt the appetite.

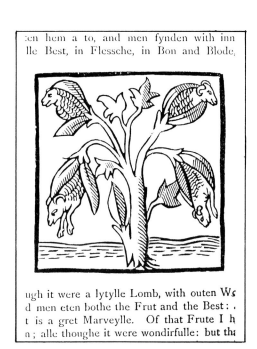

**13. Little rams bursting out of the pods of a lamb tree (Mandeville).**

The resemblance between cotton and wool in fact goes little further than a general appearance of fluffy external hairs, in contrast to the internal situation of the smoothly straight stem and leaf fibres of flax and pineapple.

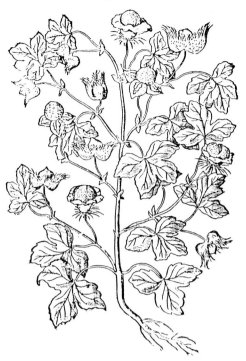

**14. The cotton tree (Matthioli).**

strengthening, during which time additional cellulose is laid down in the form of innumerable tiny spirals. When the dried-out boll cracks open, and the fluffy mass is exposed, the moisture in the centre of each fibre evaporates leaving an air-filled cavity, the lumen. At the same time the hair collapses and coils repeatedly on itself in either a right-handed or left-handed direction, achieving finally 150 or more twists per inch (fig. 16). These twists, clearly visible on the fibre surface, are a distinctive feature of cotton, as is the deep wrinkling which accompanies the reduction in size. The frequent reversal of the direction of twist along the fibre causes it to wriggle constantly as minute amounts of water are lost or regained. The function of the seed fibres, basic to the cotton industry, is probably a multiple one, serving at various times the purposes of protection, of pushing the seeds apart so that they do not fall in a lump and choke each other during growth (if natural growth were allowed that is), of absorption of water when left to germinate, and of protection from saturation if over-exposed to damp.

The hairs were formerly plucked from the seeds by hand, but the process was speeded up by the mechanical gin towards the end of the eighteenth century. The ginned cotton is called *lint*. Any remaining fragments are removed by further ginning, and are called *linters*.

The cotton tree (fig. 14), which grows to a height of about twenty feet, was cultivated for a long time, but was eventually replaced by shorter annual or biennial plants where the bolls were easier to pick and where experiments in producing new strains would yield quicker results. Unfortunately, annual cotton plants share with annual flax the compensating hazard that unfavourable weather conditions or disease can entirely wipe out a prime variety – as indeed happened with the Sea Island cotton sub-species in the 1960s.

The bolls or fruits follow on from pollination and withering of the flowers. When ripe, they contain a variable number of hard black seeds, from the skins of which extend thousands of single cells, from three-eighths to two-and-a-half inches in length according to the variety of *Gossypium* (fig. 15). The shorter fibres tend to be thicker (averaging 18 microns diameter) than the longer fibres (12 microns).

A single boll may contain 150,000 fibres or more, depending on the number of seeds which ripen. Ripening takes three weeks, and during this time the fibres gradually lengthen until each is 2000 times longer than its diameter. There follows a further three-and-a-half weeks of fibre reinforcement or

**15. A ripe cotton boll (*Everyman's Encyclopaedia, 1912*). After the flowers 'appeereth the fruit, round, and of the bignesse of a Tennise ball, wherein is thrust togither a great quantity of fine white Cotton wool; among which is wrapped up blacke seede of the bignesse of Peason, in shape like the trettles or dung of a conie' (Gerard, 1597).**

In preparation for machine spinning, the lint is beaten and exposed to rapidly revolving spiked rollers or *bale breakers*. In this way solid impurities – fragments of husk etc – are removed and the tightly packed fibres pulled apart until they are in the form of *laps*, continuous sheets of cotton wool about forty inches wide and an inch thick. *Carding* separates out the short and immature fibres. The rest proceed in the form of a filmy web or *sliver* in which the fibres lie parallel to each other, untwisted. Fibres for high quality yarns are then *combed* before several slivers together are passed through a *drawing frame* which pulls the fibres apart lengthwise into thinner groups. As further slivers are added (*slubbing*), attenuation reaches a point where a slight twist must be introduced to prevent the fibres separating completely. *Roving* thins further until, at the required fineness, the fibres are locked in position by the *spin*.

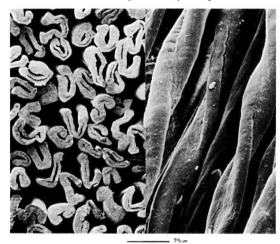

**16. Cotton fibre cells in cross-section and side view (courtesy: B.T.T.G.).**

### The secretions of Arthropods

Plant fibres are all short in comparison with those which issue from the heads of Insects and Spiders, where the silky filaments may be up to a mile in length, a difference related to the purpose which they serve.

**Silk** *Bombyx mori* (the mulberry silkworm) is the only insect of any substantial importance as far as threads of lace are concerned. Its fibrous products serve not for support, but for the enwrapment and protection of the fully grown but immature worm or larva, from which the silk of the world originates. The cocoon which it spins around itself is intended to protect it from variable humidities and tempera-tures, as well as from mechanical friction during an extended dormancy, when it gradually liquifies and then rebuilds its tissues into a moth-like form. Silk, a poor heat conductor, acts as a mini thermos flask, and cocoons in cooler climates are thicker than those in hot. Silk normally contains 10 to 12% water by weight, and can absorb up to 30%, thus the cocoon's contents cannot dry out, nor are they likely to suffer from any penetrating moisture.

The female moth is persuaded to lay her near-microscopic eggs in batches on specially-prepared cloths, to a total of 500 per moth. The eggs are so tiny that 36,000 of them weigh only one ounce.

The worms feed on mulberry leaves. Between hatching from the egg and attainment of full size, they grow thirty times bigger, from 3mm to 9cm in length, and put on weight until they are 1000 times heavier than their original 5 milligrams. The worm's thickish skin does not allow any gradual increase in size, such as occurs in ourselves. It resists expansion, so that the inner forces of its compressed bulk build up until finally the pressure ruptures the covering and the worm bursts out like a slow motion jack-in-the-box, before starting to gorge itself once more. This moulting is repeated five times in all during its feeding stage, the length of which varies with climate from approximately thirty-six days in southern China to sixty-three days in Japan.

The quantity of food consumed is enormous (it eats twice its own weight in leaves each day – try translating that into human terms) and though much of this nourishment is of course used for growth, quite a lot is converted into liquid silk (fibroin). When growth is completed, the worms stop feeding, and the liquid fibroin is extruded as two slender fila-ments which, as they issue through the single spin-neret on the head into the outside air, are hardened and stuck together by a gum, sericin, so that they form a fine strand 1000 yards or more long. Little by little the silkworm winds the strand very carefully around itself, mummy fashion, as it prepares for sleep. Over a two or three day period, the worm's content of liquid silk becomes externalized in the form of a cocoon, and its body shrinks in size. The 36,000 silkworms from one ounce of eggs will between them eat one ton of mulberry leaves. to yield finally 140 pounds weight of cocoons which in turn will provide 12 pounds of raw silk.

It is obvious that the drain on the mulberry trees could easily become excessive, and on large silk-worm farms it is quite customary to keep the eggs in cold storage, releasing them at intervals over a several months period so that they cannot, by over-

17. Stages in the refined culture of the sensitive silkworm (dedicated by J. Stradanus to Raphael Medici of Florence, 16th century).

a. The natural life cycle. Anticlockwise from top right: the moth with eggs, the worm, the cocoon, the new generation.

consumption, kill the plant which feeds them.

Shortly after the cocoons are completed, they are baked in an oven or exposed to 'live' steam, or covered with salt[20] so that the creature within is killed before it can destroy its own precious strands by emerging.

All that is needed to unwind the continuous filament of silk from the cocoons is to float them in hot water to soften the sericin, then brush them gently until the loose end is found, so that the silk can be reeled onto a rotating wheel. The cocoons are prevented from being pulled out of the water by a perforated lid, through which the filaments are threaded. The filament from a single cocoon is too fine for easy handling, so those from several cocoons, usually two to five, are picked up together and reeled at the same time, being twisted slightly in

the process. As the sericin hardens once more it cements them together as a fine thread. This gum, which may make up one-third of the total weight of the *raw silk*, causes it to look stiff and dull, and it is usually removed by, for example, boiling in soap and water (degumming), leaving a pure silk which is soft and glossy. Cleansing is followed by 'throwing' in which reeled silk is combined in various numbers and twisted in a right or left spiral according to the end-use or sink for which it is intended (figs. 17a–e).

Naturally some cocoons must be left alive to finish their development, or the insect and its profitable culture would die out in a single generation. The moths which emerge are sorry creatures: ashy-grey, mouthless, unable to feed or fly, they breed and perish, leaving the way clear for a new harvest of silk to begin.

17b. Silkworm eggs glued to the cloths where they were laid. The maiden on the right keeps them warm next to her breast, after they have been cleansed in wine. On the left, premature or unhealthy larvae are weeded out. Note the spectacles: the newly-emerged worms are extremely small.

17

17c. Wooden shelves are covered loosely with rushes to allow fresh air to enter. The human silkworm-mother must wash herself thoroughly and put on clean clothes. She should not have eaten just before tending the worms, nor handled wild chicory. Branches are brought in to construct spinning-racks for the cocoons.

17d. Mulberry leaves are gathered by the basket or sack load for the worms. Their rearing-house must be *'in a place apart, for foul smells and startling noises have a strage effect on these delicate creatures'* (Bussagli). When they finally stop eating, they are taken from their feeding trays and anchor themselves to the branches.

17e. In the centre, a bath of water is heated and the floating cocoons are brushed lightly to release their free ends. On the right, the silk is being reeled.

18a. Silk fibres in cross-section and side view (courtesy: B.T.T.G.).

**WILD SILKWORMS** also exist, but the moth cannot be domesticated or cared for, and its commercial value is far less than that of cultivated silk. *Antheraea mylitta* is a native moth of China and India. Its preferred food is not the mulberry but the dwarf oak, *Quercus serrata*. An acre of these trees can support 60,000 cocoons and provide 800 pounds of raw silk. It lives a natural if truncated life, the cocoons being collected by peasants from their outdoor hiding places, and their contents killed.

Under the microscope, differences are visible between the cultured silk, which consists of paired oval filaments encased in their lumpy gum (fig. 18a), and the wild or Tussah silk which is wedge-shaped in section with the short bases facing each other. Tussah fibres are irregular in width, and longitudinally striated.

Another wild silk, known as Anaphe, is crescent-shaped in cross-section (fig. 18b) and, like Tussah, a pale gold-brown. Neither can be reeled successfully, so they are treated as staples, and spun.

18b. Filaments of *Bombyx* (above) and *Anaphe* (below), in cross-section.

**SPIDER SILK**   While a spider is not an insect since it has the wrong number of legs and various other anatomical discrepancies, it is nevertheless reasonable closely related. Its silk is also, like that of the silkworm, concerned with a kind of embalming, though not a peaceful one. Instead, following the luring and entrapment if its prey by the glistening gossamer of its web (fig. 18c), the food is tightly wrapped in a sticky mesh of amazing strength – a bit like wrapping human food in a plastic film – so that it can be stored until needed. The piece of lace shown in fig. 18d (colour) is said to have been worked from the silk of a two-and-a-half inch long Madagascar spider.

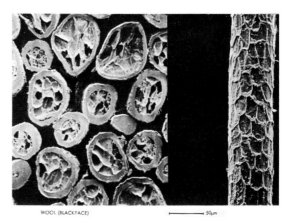

18c. *Nephila* species, the silk spider: male above, female below. Intoxication is said to accelerate production. This lacks confirmation. (courtesy: B.M.N.H.).

**Wool** is the name given to the under-hair of sheep, though the name is also applied to similar coats in other animals. Sheep ancestors, domesticated in Iraq *c*9000 BC, had a double coat. Relics from Iran between 6000 and 3000 BC indicate the gradual loss of that outer jacket and its replacement by the fine underwool grown longer to make a woolly fleece which now constitutes the wool fibres of commerce[21]. The external surface of wool and other hairs is variously crimped or waved and covered with scales (fig. 19). Wool fibres can be fine or coarse. The fine fibres of Merino – a variety thought to have been introduced into Spain by the Moors during the twelfth century, to have spread from there to other parts of Europe in the eighteenth, and to the USA and Australia in the nineteenth – have a large number of scales (2000 to the inch) and of crimps (24–30 to the inch). They are short to medium (35–90mm) and gently lustrous. The thicker wool of the Scottish blackface may be up to 300mm long[22]. The hairs have only 700 scales and 5 crimps to the inch, but the scales are irregular and protruding so that they reflect little light.

WOOL (BLACKFACE)    |⎯⎯⎯⎯⎯⎯⎯⎯⎯| 50μm

19. Wool fibres in cross-section and side view (courtesy: B.T.T.G.).

### The hairy coverings of mammals

The presence of hairs, erupting from the body surface, is a characteristic of the four-limbed, warm-blooded, milk-producing animals known as mammals, which are generally regarded as more advanced than any others. A few forms of mammalian hair have long been exploited for the construction of textiles by weaving, looping or knitting techniques and, far less commonly and much more recently, for the making of lace.

Hairs are relatively short, being staple rather than filament fibres. Their general purpose is to provide an insulating layer around the skin, keeping heat in and cold out or, in hotter areas of the globe, protecting the skin from the burning rays of the sun, for example in the kangaroo and koala.

Again, in spite of the multitude of hairy animals available, the popularity of one form outstrips all others: the sheep and its wool.

Of all the natural fibres, plant and animal, wool is the easiest to cull. In domesticated sheep it needs only to be cut off (sheared), cleaned, combed and straightened to be ready for conversion into usable thread (fig. 20). Threads made from the finest fibres are called *worsted*.

Woollen threads and fabrics contain more air than those made from other fibres since scales and crimps mean that they cannot be packed so tightly together, and this is a great advantage where warmth without weight is required, for example in lacy knitted shawls.

Like silk, which is also a protein, wool can absorb up to 30% of its weight of water and this, combined with a natural oiliness, means that except in the most torrential rain the skin below is kept dry. The property of water absorption is retained by the wool thread, though the water-repellent oiliness is removed, its beneficent qualities being outweighed by its obtrusive smell.

Sheep are convenient animals in that different varieties can flourish in all parts of the world. Other animals bearing a wool-like fleece, though theirs may be superior in quality to that of the sheep, are restricted by climatic barriers or other problems.

Hair-wise, goats are not too rigidly separated from sheep. The best fleeces come from the Angora goat of Turkey and the Cashmere goat of Tibet (figs. 21a,b).

The ANGORA GOAT is covered with ringlets of pale silky hair, up to twelve inches long. Cropped twice a year, each goat can produce between 8 and 10 pounds of fibres known as *mohair*. The small sparsely scattered scales, only about half the number of those found in fine wool, make the surface smoother and so able to reflect more light, producing a high lustre. Mohair appeared in Egypt in the seventh century AD, though it was known earlier in the Levant[23].

The CASHMERE GOAT is a native of China, northern India, Tibet, Afghanistan and Iran. It does not adapt easily to other climates, and attempts to breed it in England have failed. Unlike the modern sheep and the Angora goat, the Cashmere goat has a double layer of hair, one next to its skin of fine soft down rather like thermal underwear, and the other forming an outer protective fleece of longer coarser fibres. Each animal can provide only about 4 ounces of the coveted down per year, so that at a time of strong market demand it can command an exceptionally high price. For comparison, the fleece of a cross-bred Merino sheep may weigh up to 10 pounds[24].

The LLAMA (fig. 22) is a South American species of camel-like animal. Though some woolly laces were marketed as *lama* in the nineteenth century, they were probably made of worsted, the use of the

20. Merino-type sheep, showing the short thick fleece (Buffon, *Histoire naturelle des Mammiferes*).

21a. Cashmere goats (courtesy: B.M.N.H.).

21b. Separating the sheep from the goats. Hairs of sheep (left), goats (right).

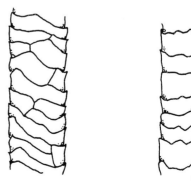

21

exotic name being simply an attempt by the merchants to add a social cachet to a fibre of strictly limited appeal. Related to the llama is the **Vicuna**. Its fleece provides the finest and rarest wool in the world. The fibres are only half the thickness of worsted and with minute scales so that they feel soft and smooth. Resistant to domestication, these tragic animals cannot be sheared, combed or plucked, and so are slaughtered in order that their coats, weighing scarcely 1 pound apiece can be taken from them.

Llama, alpaca and vicuna were all known, and woven, in twelfth-century BC Peru.

The YAK is a Tibetan ox, with long dark hair on its flanks. Like the llama it contributed its name rather than its fibres to lace, in this case to a torchon-style

23b. Yak bobbin lace, 19th century.

22. *Llama glama glama.*

23a. Tibetan yak (courtesy: B.M.N.H.).

bobbin lace made of English wool and produced in the East Midlands towards the end of the nineteenth century (figs. 23a,b).

While the woolly products of sheep and goats share a quality of softness and warmth, the hair of other mammals may be selected for quite different reasons:

**Horsehair** The hair used is not the general body covering but the longer coarser hairs, up to almost nine feet in length (fig. 24a), of the mane and tail. The hairs can be cut as required – usually during the winter when the animals have no need of them to brush away flies – and their preparation is minimal. Their thickness and stiffness readily distinguish them from other mammalian fibres used for threads of lace.

**Cow hairs** have probably never been used for lace as such but in earlier times they were made into strainers using a looping technique similar to certain stitches appearing almost universally in needle laces[25] (fig. 24b).

**Human hair** from the head could possibly rival the length of the Prince Imperial's mane if allowed to grow until its weight and unmanageability became an embarrassment to the owner. Like that of the horse it has simply to be cut and cleaned to be ready for use.

24a. The Prince Imperial, c1870, held the world record for his 8ft 10in length of mane (from the Harry T. Peters *America on Stone* lithography collection. Smithsonian Institution).

24b. Cow. The longest hairs are plucked from the tail (Buffon).

Table 2

| FIBRE ASPECT | LINEN | COTTON | SILK | WOOL | REGENERATED | SYNTHETIC |
|---|---|---|---|---|---|---|
| Source | Plant / Flax (*Linum*) / Bast of stem | Plant / Cotton (*Gossypium*) / Seed hairs | Animal / (*Bombyx*) / Cocoon | Animal / Sheep (*Ovis*) / Skin hairs | Plant eg viscose rayon (cotton linters); Animal eg lanital, ardil, vicara (milk, ground nut, maize) | Fossils eg in petroleum or coal eg nylon |
| Form of occurence | Bundles of fibres (staple) | Single fibres (staple) | Double strand (filament) | Single (staple) | Single (filament) | Usually single, may be double (filament) |
| Chemical nature | Cellulose plus 2% lignin | Cellulose | Protein: fibroin + seracin (no sulphur) | Protein: keratin (sulphur) | Cellulose or globular protein | polyamides polyesters acrylics etc. |
| External features | Nodes | Ribbon-like spiralling in alt. directions | Smooth | Scales and crimps | Rayon: longitudinal grooves | Smooth |
| Length of fibres (over a range of varieties) | Raw fibres: 5-20 in. 12.7 - 50.8 cm. ultimates 1.6-2.4mm | 0.75-2.25 in. 1.9-5.8 cm. | Usually 1000-1300 yd. (915 - 1190 m.) (up to 3000 m.) | 1.5-15 in. 3.8-38 cm. | No natural limit to filament length, but can be made into staples | |
| Length in proportion to width (average) | x 1200 | x 1400 | x 33,000,000 | x 3000 | Can be varied by manufacturer | |

# 5 Other fibre features

Fibres exist because of their usefulness to the plant and animal sources which bore, or contained, them. Their whole chemical structure and all their physical features are directed to the original role they were created to perform.

It is purely coincidental that those same features give them, in the world of man, a practical commercial value, and that that value can be exploited towards the economic end of lace manufacture.

### II. VRTICA. II.

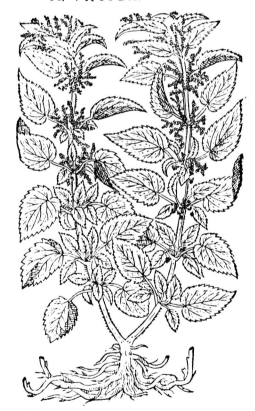

**25a.** Nettle, *Urtica dioica*, (Matthioli). Spun and woven nettle fibres were used by one of the earliest people on earth, the Ainu, or hairy aborigines of Japan, and they have been found on Egyptian mummies of 2050 BC.

In chapters 2 and 3, the chemical and physical aspects of fibres in relation to their natural occurence was explored. In moving on to their detachment from these sources, and their application to a new and quite different usefulness, the relevant features are no longer concerned with support and protection, but with profitability. How will the fibres/threads look, how will they feel, how will they behave? Will they stretch? Do they shine? Will they absorb water? How strong are they? Do they shrink? Are they cold or warm, light or heavy, clear or fluffy, hard or soft? Are they harmed by light, insects, acids, friction, age? What is their natural colour? Do they accept dyes? Do they stain?

Unfortunately, for the purposes of scientific statement, all these qualities tend to be assessed in rather esoteric terms such as elongation at break, moisture regain, tensile strength, elastic recovery, dimensional stability, abrasion resistance, flammability behaviour and thermal conductivity. Their precise determination requires extreme accuracy, the testing of many samples taken at random to avoid chance selection of an atypical form, and the use of professional techniques and equipment, full details of which are far beyond the scope of this book or, one would imagine, the facilities available to most of its readers. Table 3 is a simplified summary containing some generalized measurements obtained by such means. They are intended to be comparative rather than absolute.

### Other plant fibres used for laces

Stem and leaf fibres which have occasionally been used for laces will be listed briefly here. Their varying qualities help to explain why so few were ever of outstanding importance, and why none ever posed any serious competition to the pre-eminence of flax.

**Bast fibres** of antiquity such as ramie, nettle, jute and hemp, are basically similar to flax in their nature, and in their arrangement within the stem (figs. 25a,b).

**RAMIE** (*Boehmeria nivea*, also known as Rhea or China Grass) belongs to a family of stingless nettles, and is mostly obtained from China. Because of the amount of gum around them, the fibres are difficult to extract. The stems must be beaten vigorously to break the cambial layer and enable the outer cylinder or cortex to be peeled away from the woody core (decortication). The inner surface of the cortex is then softened by soaking in water, and scraped with a knife or the semi-sharp edge of a shell, until the fibre-groups can be pulled out as long ribbons. This is called *degumming*: the fibres become unstuck. The process is similar to that described for pineapple fibres (p. 13). After further soaking and scraping, sometimes assisted by alkalis of soda or lime, the groups of fibres can be split lengthwise until they are fine enough for practical use. Extraction was mechanized in the 1960s, reducing the cost of production.

It is however no modern discovery, and Egyptian mummies swathed in woven ramie date from 5000 to 3300 BC. In the Middle Ages it was used by Mediterranean peoples, and it extended from there through much of western Europe[26]. Like linen, ramie is strong, white, lustrous and durable. It absorbs water readily but, unlike linen, dyes easily. Its fibres however are coarser, and the great variation in length of its ultimates (from 50 to 200 mm) makes it impossible to separate them into really fine strands. Thus they have a low spinning quality, and tend to produce a softly shaggy yarn. Ramie can be mercerized in the same way as cotton.

**NETTLE** (*Urtica dioica*, the stinging nettle, and other species). Relics of nettle fibre date back to 2000 BC in Egypt and to the early Bronze Age in Scandinavia where it is known as Swedish hemp. *Urtica* is a herbaceous perennial. The upright stalks which bear the leaves and flowers die back each year, while the underground stem persists and ramifies to send up new shoots the following spring. The fibres are released by retting, followed by boiling and hackling. They are creamy-white, soft and lustrous, but not very strong, and the yield per plant is low, as might be expected from its restricted size, and it has never achieved any significant economic importance.

**JUTE** (*Corchorus*) grows best in hot damp areas, particularly India. The plant is a 15 foot high annual with stems three-quarters of an inch in diameter. Retting is followed by an easy separation of the fibre strands, which are sometimes 7 feet in length, though the ultimates measure only one-tenth of an inch. The fibres are pleasingly lustrous, but their colour is yellowish-brown to grey, and they darken when exposed to light. The 20% lignin content makes them stiff and inelastic and, as in ramie, the tips tend to spring out from the yarn as it dries, giving the threads a rough hairy texture more appropriate to sackcloth than lace.

**HEMP** (*Cannabis sativa*) is a large annual plant, growing to a height of 10 feet or more. Its fibres are extracted in a manner similar to flax. From the point of view of lace, they combine the disadvantages of ramie (the extracted fibres are long but the ultimates minute) and of jute (a high lignin content makes them hard, stiff and inflexible). Hemp has been found in Neolithic fragments from Switzerland, worked in a looping stitch similar to those used in historic needle laces.

The plant probably originated in the Far East, and it is recorded in China nearly 5000 years ago[27]. In northern India the wild form was valued as a source of hashish, not fibres. Hemp was, incidentally, one of the yarns listed among the prohibitions of the Burial in Woollen Acts of 1667 and 1678, where an official witness had to attest that the 'lately deceased' was not 'put in, wrapt or wound up or buried in any shirt, shift, sheet or shroud made or mingled with flax, hemp, silk, hair, gold or silver, or other than what is made of sheep's wool only . . .'

**25b. Hemp, *Cannabis* (Dalechamps).**

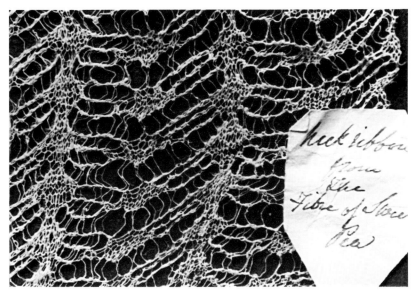

SWEET PEA (*Lathyrus odorata*).    The lace illustrated in fig. 25c is said to have been knitted from Sweet Pea fibres. Although there is no record of this fibre having been used commercially, Sunn hemp (*Crotalaria juncea*), which has considerable economic importance, belongs to the same family of flowering plants (*Leguminosae*).

**Leaf fibres**

SISAL (*Agave sisalana*).    Fig. 25d shows a piece of Tenerife-style lace reputedly made of fibres from this Central American plant. It has a very short trunk bearing a crown of leaves, which are harvested at intervals during the seven years of its useful life, each leaf providing up to 1000 fibres.

25c. Detail of a scarf knitted with fibres said to be from the sweet pea. Microscopically, they are more like *Cannabis*.

Both *Agave* and *Yucca* textiles, dating from around 2000 BC, have been found in Peru[28]. The succulent flesh of the leaves is pounded or scraped away and the fibres drawn beneath the teeth to cleanse them further. Yucca thread, is usually spun S plyed Z (see ch. 6), and may be nearly one-eighth of an inch in diameter.

25d. A lace of Teneriffe-style work, probably made of raffia, the outer layer or epidermis of the leaf of the *Raphia* palm.

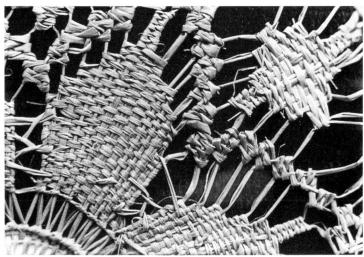

**Table 3**                         OTHER FIBRE FEATURES

Note: Numbers given in the various sections are arranged in the order:   linen (L), cotton (C), silk (S), wool (W), regenerated (R), synthetic (SY). Except where otherwise stated, R is viscose rayon, and SY nylon 6.6. Measurements quoted by different authorities can vary considerably, depending on the method used to obtain them.

**Strength** (tensile strength or tenacity): Fibres must be strong enough to be made into yarns and then into lace. In effect their strength is a measure of how much strain they can take, expressed as weight per unit area, i.e. pounds per square inch or grams per denier. The minimum required is 2.5 gm/denier, but in wool elasticity compensates for weakness. In yarns, their strength is a measure of their ability to hold together under the stresses they must suffer, for example during the vigorous working of the lace machines. Conversion of cotton into yarn reduces its strength, since the short staples can be pulled apart; in wool, the scales and crimping help the fibres to cling together, and the yarn is relatively stronger.
gm/den:

L. 4.5-6.3 (wet, 20% stronger);          C. 2.3-4.5 (wet, 20% stronger);
S. 2.4-5.0 (wet, 20% weaker);            W. 1.1-1.7 (weaker when wet eg 0.8);
R. 1.5-4.0 (wet, 0.9-1.5);               SY. 4.1-5.5
--------------------------------------------------------------------------------

**Specific gravity**: This is one of the factors which determines whether the lace feels light or heavy. It is a measure of density, not in a direct relation of volume to mass, but as a multiple of the density of water, which for this purpose is taken as 1. Thus a specific gravity of 1.5 means that the fibre is one-and-a-half times as heavy as an equal volume of water.
L. 1.54;   C. 1.54;   S. 1.3;   W. 1.32; R. 1.52; SY. 1.14
--------------------------------------------------------------------------------

**Water absorption** (moisture regain): The proportion of the fibre's total weight which can consist of absorbed water or, more accurately, the weight of water absorbed under experimental conditions, divided by the total weight of the dry fibre, and multiplied by 100. In laces, it is linked to the acceptance of dyes, and also to strength since linen and cotton are stronger when wet, while silk, wool and rayon are weaker.
%age of dry weight:
L. 12%, yarns do not shrink or stretch;
C. 8.5%, max. absorption 25%, may shrink;
S. 11%, max. 30%, yarns do not shrink or stretch;
W. 13-16%, max. 30%, yarns tend to felt;
R. 13%, yarns swell and stretch;
SY. 3.5-5.0%, yarns keep their shape.
--------------------------------------------------------------------------------

**Stretchability** (extension at break): Technically, this is how far a fibre can be stretched in a straight line before it breaks, measured as a percentage of its original length.
L. dry 1%, wet 2.2-3.3%;               C. 3.0-7.0%;
S. 10-25%, wet 33%;                    W. dry 25-30%, wet up to 50%;
R. dry 10-25%, wet 23-32%;             SY. dry 26-32%, wet 30-40%;
Elastomeric 500%.
--------------------------------------------------------------------------------

**Elasticity/stiffness** : (elastic recovery or resistance to deformation): is also related to lengthening. It is measured in terms of the extent to which a fibre returns to its original size and shape when stretched repeatedly to 2% longer than normal, and expressed as a percentage. This feature is important during both manufacture and handling: if the elastic recovery is low, the lace may crease or be pulled out of shape. It is also more likely to break under tension.
L. 65%; C. 75%; S. 92%; W. 99%; R. 82%; SY. 100%.
--------------------------------------------------------------------------------

**Bendability** (flexibility, pliability): the previous two features relate to stretching in a straight line. Bendability refers to the sideways curving of the fibre, a process of bending without breaking. It expresses the ability of the fibre to return to its original position after localised compression. Even limited flex can bestow on the lace an attractive *drape*, enabling it to hang gracefully and to flow with the body's movements, though the total effect is strongly influenced by the density of the fibres (depending on their chemical nature), of the yarn (depending on the tightness of the spin), and of the lace itself (depending on the compactness or otherwise of its working).

L. Sympathetically constructed, the fabric appears supple, but the fibres themselves have a high degree of firmness and their strength is quickly reduced by repeated bending. This is something to remember when storing laces.

C. Fairly inflexible, creases easily.

S. Supple.                          W. Very resilient, springy.

R. Fairly supple.                   SY. More flexible at higher temperatures.

**Resilience** is the effect of the last three features combined.

---------------------------------------------------------------------------------------------------------------------------------

**Spinning quality** or cohesiveness: means the ability of the fibres to hold together when spun or twined. Scales and spiralling convolutions help them to adhere, while longer fibres are more easily bound, their length permitting more twists to be inserted per fibre.

---------------------------------------------------------------------------------------------------------------------------------

**Lustre** (gloss, sheen or shine) is a measure of the amount of light reflected from the yarn surface. In general, the smoother the surface, the higher the lustre. A very tight spin or ply tends to reduce lustre; so does over-retting; or the presence of impurities such as gums.

L. High, due to a thin layer of wax on the fibre surface. This is often polished by friction or heat in the finished lace. May have a silky sheen, *cf* gimp threads in earlier bobbin laces.

C. Low, appears dull because its convolutions give an irregular surface.

S. High, but much depends on the spin. Spun silk is less glossy than reeled.

W. Related to size and protuberance of scales, depth of crimps, and diameter of fibres. See Table 4.

R. Dull to bright, controlled by manufacturer.

SY. Extremely smooth. Excessive brightness can be delustred.

---------------------------------------------------------------------------------------------------------------------------------

**Colour**: All fibres are mainly white or off-white in their natural state, and those which are not may be made white by bleaching. All except linen are easily dyed.

L. Light bisque through pale yellow to dark tan, and steel- or pearl-grey. Tints are affected by different retting procedures.

C. May be cream or brown.

S. Shades of pale to dark gold.

W. Occasionally gray, brown or black. Earlier sheep were speckled, and the long coarse wool of the wild llama was 'white, grey or russet disposed in spots' (Buffon).

R. and SY. White, but easily dyed.

---------------------------------------------------------------------------------------------------------------------------------

**Visual texture** (clear/clean/sharp versus fluffy/cloudy/obscure):

L. Clear and clean when long line fibres are used but, with shorter tow fibres , the effect is similar to cotton.

C. Fluffiness increases with shortness of staple and poorer quality of yarn.

S. Gleaming and smooth.

W. Worsted yarn fairly sharp when new, becoming cloudy with wear.

R. Clear.

SY. Clear, as a filament, slightly fluffy when spun as a staple.

---------------------------------------------------------------------------------------------------------------------------------

**Effect of friction**   (abrasion resistance): All lacemaking techniques involve considerable friction and chosen yarns must not be weakened by this.

Resistance:   L.  Fair to good;       C.   Fair to good, but fluff increases;
              S.  Good;             W.  Good;
              R.  Better than cotton;   SY.  Excellent resistance.

---

**Thermal and electrical conductivity**: these determine whether the lace feels cool or warm, and whether it produces static charges.

Conductivity:   L.  Good, feels cool to cold.
               C.  Fair, feels coolish, but air content of fibres reduces conductivity.
               S.  Poor, feels warm, and produces static.
               W.  Air content of yarn resulting from the uneven fibre surface makes it warm, and a good insulator.
               R.  Good, little static.
               SY.  Poor.  Lack of water absorption causes a build-up of huge amounts of static, and suppressors must be fitted to the machines which wind synthetic yarns onto spools or brass bobbins for lace manufacture.  The fibres may feel cold and clammy.

---

**Effect of light**: Light has a destructive action on all lace fibres, through providing energy for chemical reactions which cause deterioration.  Linen is less susceptible than cotton, but in both the degree of polymerisation is reduced and some yellowing occurs due to oxidation.  Silk, especially if it has been 'weighted' after degumming, undergoes slow disintegration and shattering.  In wool, strong light decomposes the keratin, even while still on the sheep: the sulphur is converted to sulphuric acid which reacts with alkalis, increasing the destructive action of soap, soda, borax, ammonia and sodium hypochlorite.  Ultra-violet light harms regenerated and synthetic fibres.

---

**Effects of acids and alkalis**: Cellulose fibres are resistant to alkalis, but easily harmed by acids which gradually cause decomposition of the insoluble cellulose into soluble glucose.  Protein fibres are resistant to weak acids, though harmed by strong; wool in particular is attacked by alkalis.

Regenerated cellulose is disintegrated by strong acids and alkalis, but unharmed by weak.  Synthetics may dissolve in acids, alkalis have no effect.

---

**Attacks by insects** (moths, carpet beetles, silverfish): linen and cotton are not attacked, unless they have been stored with starch (food) still in them.  Silk is destroyed by carpet beetles.  Wool is edible to all.  Viscose rayon is eaten by silverfish.  Synthetics contain no nourishment, but may be attacked by ants and cockroaches.

---

**Attacks by micro-organisms** (fungi and bacteria): In damp conditions, linen, cotton and rayons are fed on by mildews and decay bacteria which rot them by digesting the cellulose.  Silk and wool are more resistant.  Synthetics have a very high resistance.

---

**Effect of age** (capacity for survival): Yarns and fabrics of linen, cotton and wool have survived from the Stone Age, many thousands of years ago, but their ability to do so depends on the absence of the harmful factors listed above.  Silk survives less well, attacked in many instances by the mordants used to dye it.  Man-made fibres have existed for less than 100 years, and it is too early to attempt a reliable prognosis.

---

# 6 Fibres make threads

26. Spinning with a distaff: (i) Expelled from the Garden of Eden, Eve spins thread for a gown. *St Mary's Psalter*, c1320 (by permission of The British Library).

Quite short lengths of fibre, just the amount in fact that will fit conveniently into a sewing needle, can be used to produce small functional objects by a looping movement (see fig. 43f). In antiquity, it was the practise for new lengths to be added one at a time as they were needed, the new being spliced or knotted to the old, so that thread-making and fabric construction proceeded smoothly, one alternating with the other in a continuous manner. Thick fibres such as horsehair or human hair, known as monofilaments, could be used in this way; so could thin slices of animal skin, chewed sinews, slivers of tree bark or the straight wiry veins of leaves.

However, the later development of weaving required greater lengths of smoother strands, and some quite different approach to making a thread became necessary. A sufficient quantity had to be prepared before, not during, use.

The simplest method of doing this was to extend the process of splicing, repeating it time after time, and winding the resultant yardage into a ball. This was called *twining*. It consisted of rolling the fibres along the thigh or shin with the palm of the hand, and with the ends overlapped slightly so that they held together. The movement could be in either direction, from knee to hip producing a clockwise turn, and from hip to knee an anti-clockwise. The skin might be encased in a plaster of clay, or rubbed with ashes, to prevent soreness from the recurrent friction[29].

The seniority and skill of this technique are indicated by the murals of Egyptian tombs nearly 5000 years old (see fig. 2), by clay models of similar age, and by surviving fragments of cloth which are not only finely woven but demonstrate that plying or doubling of the threads had already been mastered. From the Middle East, c1250 BC, come references to the luxurious vestments woven for Aaron from 'fine twined linen'.

Although twining is still practised by a number of nomadic peoples in warmer lands today, in Transjordan and the Sudan for example, greater control over the fibres can be achieved by replacing the leg with the hands, in a series of movements known as *spinning*. This consists essentially of making the fibres spin, or rotate, on their own axes, several at a time, so that they spiral around each other and cling together in a stable manner.

This more sophisticated method of converting fibres into threads can be separated into three distinct operations: attenuation (called *drafting* or *drawing out*), turning, and winding.

26(ii). A French lady, c1700.

Twining certainly preceded spinning in age, and can still be a preliminary to its action. More usually, however, the fibres undergo a lengthy preparation which ends with the formation of a *rove*. This is a loosely compacted mass which may be held in the hand or mounted on a support, the *distaff*, which is often just a stick, or a simple frame. Fibres are plucked from the distaff and eased smoothly out until, the desired degree of slenderness having been attained, the spinner turns them with her thumb, curling them lengthwise around each other (fig. 26). Drawing and turning follow a harmonious sequence so that, however fine the yarn may become, the fibres are made to hold together and the yarn does not break.

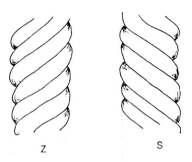

Z          S

27. Spiralling fibres together to make a yarn, the two possible directions.

The direction of the turn may be either clockwise or anti-clockwise. Initially, these terms relate to the movement of the spinner's thumb, a movement to the right producing an anti-clockwise twisting motion, and to the left a clockwise. The effect which these two motions have on the yarn is shown in fig. 27.

However, if the spun yarn itself is looked at from either end, and the turning of the fibres continued, they will be seen to go in a clockwise or right-handed direction in the first example, and in the reverse way for the second. A similar contradiction exists in machine-spinning. If the flyer is looked at from above, its anti-clockwise turning (left), will be seen to produce a clockwise or right-handed spin. Yet this is sometimes referred to as a left-spin, since the fibres themselves now lie in the same direction as in a left-handed screw[30].

The actual movements which produced these turns cannot of course be seen in the finished yarn and, since both clockwise and anti-clockwise, as well as the terms right and left, are obviously subject to misinterpretation, the letters S and Z are substituted in description, the central stroke of each letter indicating a clearly visible direction which cannot be disputed. This nomenclature was first adopted in 1937, by the International Cotton Committee[31]. The directions described above can easily be checked by taking two thin pieces of plastic-covered wire, holding them together at one end and rotating them around each other, on the leg or by the thumb, to produce an S or a Z twist. Their clockwise and anti-clockwise aspects can then be investigated.

The twist initiated by the spinner's fingers was reinforced, and eventually replaced, by an implement known as the *spindle*. Primitively this was no more than the rib of a palm leaf, or a thin stalk of reed or bamboo.

The spindle can be manipulated in a variety of ways. It may be held, supported on the ground by a fragment of shell or gourd, or allowed to hang free (figs. 28, 29): In this latter method, referred to as a drop-, or suspended-spindle it may be set rotating by a sharp turn along the spinner's thigh, continuing to spin as it hangs. Except when the spindle is actually held in the hand, a small weight or *whorl* made of bone, wood, clay, or even – in a more temporary manner – a fruit or potato, is attached to steady it. When the spindle is dropped, the whorl stretches the yarn by its weight, making it even more slender. These primitive spinning techniques, admirably suited to a life involving outdoor wanderings, spread northwards from Egypt, reaching Britain by the time of the Roman Iron Age, *c*200 AD.

29. Suspended spindle in Ancient Greece *(Daremberg)*.

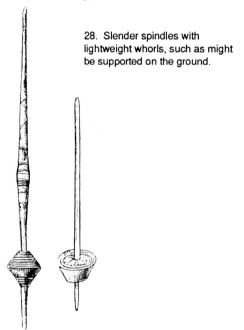

28. Slender spindles with lightweight whorls, such as might be supported on the ground.

Rather later, and probably between 500 and 1000 AD, in India, a fourth method of spinning evolved, using a simple machine, the *spinning wheel*[32] (fig. 30). By the end of the thirteenth century, it was being welcomed in northern Europe by a society increasingly preoccupied with speed and the acquisition of money, values totally at variance with the slow timelessness of nomadic existence. The wheel may however have been too expensive for general use, and Fiennes during her travels *Through England on a Side-saddle* in 1698, noted that: 'the ordinary people both in Suffolk and Norfolk knitt much and spin, some with the rock and fusoe as the French does' (*fuseau* is the French for bobbin or spindle; the

rock is the distaff). The early European wheel, known as the Long wheel or Great wheel (fig. 31), was used for wool in England and Ireland, and for hemp in Holland. Two hands were needed, one to turn the wheel which rotated the spindle, the other to draw out and twist the rove. Improvements about 1530 were followed by the addition of a treadle to produce the Brunswick wheel, leaving both hands free to draw and twist with increasing acceleration, until a contemporary merchant complained that the spinners were so carried away by the rocking of their feet that they allowed all kinds of irregularities in the yarn to slip through their fingers.

The process of winding-on is equally important. In the prehistoric twining of linen, the spliced fibre strands were wound into a ball. In hand-spinning, the spindle serves a dual purpose, rotating to turn the fibres, and forming an axis onto which the spun yarn can be wound. In the *intermittent* or discontinuous technique, the spinner has to stop twisting in order to wind, this latter being done with great care to avoid distorting the freshly-made yarn.

In the late fifteenth century, a *flyer* was invented which allowed *continuous* winding on of the yarn as it was spun. This produced the Saxony or Flax wheel (fig. 32).

When advanced mechanization began in the eighteenth century, the processes of drawing out, of twisting and of winding did not alter in principle. The change was in the number of yarns (up to 2800) that could be spun at the same time by one person

30. An Indian spinning wheel, drawn by J.L.Kipling (courtesy: V and A).

31. The Great Wheel, *Standing Spinner* by J.F.Millet (courtesy: Museum of Fine Arts, Boston).

and, eventually, in the greatly increased speed (up to 11,000 revolutions per minute) at which the whole thing progressed[33]. Indeed statistics of cotton yarn production from this time onwards often quote numbers of spindles in use rather than numbers of machines. In 1860 for example, 36 million spindles were in operation, kept in motion by steam or water power. In one minute they could spin enough cotton yarn to encircle the earth four times. By 1912, there were over 140 million spindles in the world, 40% of them in the United Kingdom[34].

The earliest successful machine was Hargreaves' Spinning Jenny (or engine) patented in 1770 which, beginning with 8 spindles, progressed to 16 and then 30. It regressed however to the pre-flyer technique, drawing and twisting alternating with winding on, instead of proceeding simultaneously.

Since all the main spinning machine developments were connected with cotton, they will be considered in that section (p. 39).

The product of the first spin is known as a *single* (once-spun or single-spun yarn). A second spin, known as *doubling*, *folding*, *plying* or *twisting*, can combine two or more yarns into one thread, by rotating them either in the same direction as before, giving a tighter or harder twist; or in the reverse direction, giving a looser or softer twist (fig. 33).

The precise method used to spin a particular fibre has to be adapted to suit its chemical and physical properties such as its length, its need for moisture, and its capacity for association with other similar fibres.

34

32. The Saxony wheel in the foreground. In the background sowing, stacking, rippling, braking, scutching and hackling are all shown; on the right is the weaver with his loom; on the left, the bleachfield, and beside it the retting stream.

## Linen

The preparation of the fibres up to the point where they are ready for spinning has been indicated in chapter 4. The initial extraction of flax and other internal plant fibres is a tedious, expensive and skilled process, but the care bestowed at those stages contributes greatly to the quality in the final product, and once the bundles of fibres have been separated from the other stem tissues and split into smaller groups, the long strands are fairly easily converted into yarn.

Evidence for antique methods of spinning may be discovered as decorations of artefacts, for example on an ancient Greek vase (see fig. 29), where a spinner is shown holding a small drop-spindle, the rove from the distaff passing through her mouth before being drawn out and twisted by her fingers into yarn. It is essential that the finer flax fibres are kept moist as they are spun, or they will become brittle. The spiralling of the wet yarn as it dries will reinforce or tighten an S-spin, engendered by the fingers and aided by the rotating spindle. The practice of using spit to wet the flax is again illustrated in one of the tales, possibly dating back to the seventeenth century, collected in Germany by the Brothers Grimm during the first half of the nineteenth century. In *The Three Spinners*, one has a huge right foot from 'treading' (pressing the treadle of the spinning wheel), a second an underlip so distorted that it hangs down over her chin, and the third a broad left thumb from 'twisting'. The underlip was got by 'licking', that is by repeatedly licking the thumb or by passing the rove through the mouth so that the warm wetness of the saliva saves the fibres from desiccation and also softens the gum that holds them in their bundles, so that they can be drawn out more easily, making a finer thread.

The fineness of the yarns produced depends partly on the age of the plant from which the fibres were extracted (the older the tougher), and partly on the extent to which the bast fibres are separated. Each bundle contains up to forty fibres composed lengthways of individual cells, or ultimates, which have a minimum length of 1.6 and a maximum of 24 millimetres. The greater the splitting up of the bundles during hackling, the thinner and frailer and more prone to disintegration into their ultimate parts will the strands become.

33. Plying: two yarns twisted together to make a thread.

two Z-spun singles plyed S

35

To make the superfine yarns of the late seventeenth and the eighteenth centuries, extremely careful retting would be essential, indeed every stage of the preparation for spinning would need the most skilful and patient supervision to prevent the fragile attachment of the ultimates to each other from being ripped apart. As for the spinning itself, the utmost skill of the spinner's art would be required to prevent splitting of the delicately held and almost invisible yarn as she drew out the minutely selected groups of fibres from the rove and twisted them gently yet firmly together. The slowness of drawing out and the twist intervals would have to be judged by an educated sensitivity of touch, or an experienced muscle-memory, rather than by sight, requiring a breath-holding patience of concentration and a stillness of movement such that no stirring of the air or miniscule abruptness of action could jar and break the precious yarn. Nor is it likely that such a frail rove could be taken through the mouth without the risk of body heat softening the glue too much so that the fibres would fall apart into fragments. The spinners therefore had to be as it were encapsulated in moisture, enveloped by the cool dank humidity of cellars in summer, or the moist smelly warmth of cow byres in winter – and perhaps only a total dedication, or desperation, could have enabled them to endure. In the eighteenth century, spinsters are said to have been paid a higher wage than lacemakers, and the cost of their finest count yarn was priced at several times an equal weight of pure gold.

An S-spin may seem natural and advantageous, the outer fibrils of the flax fibre being arranged in S-spirals, and it is certainly characteristic of the woven linens of ancient Egypt as well as of many linen yarns used in antique European laces (see p. 41), but the reverse or Z-twist also occurs, particularly for weaving or in heavier threads, for example in the nineteenth-century embroidered lace, Hedebo, from Denmark, and in woven linens from Greece[36]. Since flax fibres – looking at the free end – spiral in a Z-direction as they absorb moisture, and in an S-direction as they dry, a Z-spun thread will unwind as it dries, producing a softer, but also a weaker, more tenuously held together, fabric.

Peruvian linens may also show a Z-twist and the following observations were made in 1952 by Bird and Mahler:

'Interest . . . has led us to check on the direction of twist used in spinning bast fibre among American Indian tribes, with the result that there appears to be a distinct distribution of the two possibilities. North of the equator, the general practise seems to have been to twist them clockwise, while south of this line the reverse is true. Does this reflect the action of sunlight on plant growth? Such flax and other fibres we have checked show a basic difference, the southern samples twisting in opposite direction to the northern ones when moistened. The implication is that if we wish to produce linen yarn of the same quality, flax grown in the southern hemisphere must be spun in opposite manner to the practise for northern hemisphere flax.'

There is no quarrel here with the general reversal of natural forces in the two hemispheres, which results from their different relations to the sun and to the centre of the earth (both of which are to the south in the northern hemisphere and to the north in the southern hemisphere), so that clockwise north of the equator automatically becomes anti-clockwise south of that line – and even the vortex of bathwater sucked away down the plughole reverses its direction of swirl (clockwise in the north, anti-clockwise in the south) once the Line has been crossed. It is worth noting that, at least in Europe, flax, ramie and nettle rotate S during drying, while hemp and most other bast fibres rotate Z.

The diminishing availability of truly fine linen yarn, from the mid-eighteenth century onwards, probably arose from a variety of causes – the loss, by infestation, of a prime variety of flax plant, flax being particularly susceptible to fungal disease as well as to attacks from the flax beetle and from a parasitic plant known as dodder which injects suckers into the inner tissues of the roots, robbing them of nourishment. Changes in climate may also have played a part; or the false economy of leaving the plants to mature and so produce more, but thicker, fibres; impoverishment of the soil; or the insidious introduction of retting with chemicals, and of scutching and hackling by machine, which only relatively gross fibres could survive. But the major cause must quite simply have been economic: the cost of production. Profit was the very heartbeat which kept the lace industry alive. Competition from more quickly made, less expensive, and more showily effective silk laces after 1760, and the continually diminishing cost of machine-spun cotton yarn led, in the later eighteenth century, to a reduction in demand for fine linens. According to Ashworth, in 1786 a pound of 100s cotton cost 38 shillings (£1.90); and 1860 only 2s 6d (25p); while during the same period, the cost of cotton dress material fell from 6s (30p) a yard to one-thirtieth of that amount[37].

Ultra-fine spinning had an extremely slow production rate. As with the most diaphanous of laces, there was no way this tender art could be hastened. Acceleration of human spinners and human lacemakers can be achieved only by increasing the yarn thickness. Inevitably the market for the superlative shrank; the spinners of fragile yarns lost through non-use their skill; wages eventually rose and, with that, the production of the flax gossamers of the early 1700s became a commercial impossibility.

The machine-spinning of flax lagged far behind that of cotton, and the mechanization of the various stages of its difficult and lengthy preparation resulted in a coarsening and shortening of its fibre strands (for example by cutting the plant stems instead of pulling them up by the roots), and the production of inferior threads since the more delicate fibres could not survive the process. This in turn raised cotton to the position of an upmarket yarn in all except a few areas, such as England, where cotton was easily and cheaply available, while linen was the harder-to-grow, more expensive and therefore more highly desirable fibre, expecially in view of its strong link with antiquity and its use by the upper crust of society.

The gill frame was invented in the early nineteenth century by Philippe de Girard, in response to Napoleon I's offer in 1810 of one million francs for the invention of the best machinery for spinning flax. Girard did not get his reward, since Napoleon was quickly preoccupied with other things; and neither were his machines (for wet and for dry methods) a commercial success. Instead it was an English invention, first patented in 1787 which, through successive improvements, eventually established the industry. Dry-spinning produced only an irregular thickish yarn, useless for lace. The vital presence of water was made possible in 1814 when a wet-spinning process for coarse thread was introduced. It was much improved in 1825 when the entire rove was passed through a bath of hot water, equivalent to the be-spitalled mouth of the human spinner. This served a dual purpose since flax fibres are up to 20% stronger when wet and so are better able to withstand the rather brash machine treatment, while by softening the gum and washing away extraneous materials it allowed the fibres to be drafted smoothly into more slender groups, making a superior quality thread. But there was still no comparison whatsoever between these and the almost superhuman entrancements of more than a century before. The first Irish spinning mill was established in 1828. The idea was quickly pirated by the French who set up mills in Lille in 1835.

Tow could be spun in a manner similar to cotton, for example on the Mule, producing a Z-twist yarn.

### Pineapple

The extremely fine leaf fibres of the pineapple plant have a low lignin content, and they are lustrous, flexible and strong, though too resilient to submit in any docile manner to the normal processes of drawing and twisting, or even to twining. The extracted fibres, fifteen inches to three feet in length, are selected, one at a time, and lowered coil-like into a jar. The end is then tied to the next fibre, base to base or tip to tip, which gives the yarn slightly varying diameters but greater strength. The loose ends of the overhand knots (fig. 34a) are trimmed back with sharpened bamboo so that in the beautifully woven piña cloth they are scarcely visible[38]. Neither the preparation of the yarn nor the weaving of the cloth has, to date, been mechanized.

34a. An overhand knot.

### Cotton

Cotton fibres have two advantages over linen. Firstly, they are external, so that no retting, hackling or scutching are necessary. Secondly, they are totally separate from each other, instead of being held together in bundles.

Cotton however has its own problems, namely the extremely tenacious attachment of the fibres to the seed, so that they are difficult to separate. Nevertheless some of the finest fabrics ever created were made of fibres plucked by hand direct from the seed of the wild tree cotton. Preserved in their original order, they were immediately drawn and twisted into a smooth, durable yarn using a drop spindle and whorl weighing no more than 4 or 5 grams[39]. For commercial purposes, however, this hand picking away of the fibres was appallingly slow and, even with slave labour, time was money. A slightly quicker method was to use a *roller gin* or *churka* (fig. 34b). This rather primitive implement resembled a miniature wringer, or a crimping iron, two rollers being turned against each other by a handle. While the cotton fibres passed between the rollers, the seeds were arrested, and their attachments severed with a knife blade.

**34b. A churka, by J.L.Kipling (courtesy: V and A).**

The real breakthrough came in 1793 when Eli Whitney, in the USA, invented the *saw gin*, which ripped off the seeds with great rapidity. It was however too vigorous for the long-stapled fibres of Sea Island and Egyptian cottons, which continued to be de-seeded by the roller, itself eventually mechanized. It has been estimated that is took between 26 and 30 hours to pluck the fibres from one pound of seeds by hand; while by the roller gin, 40 to 65 lbs could be plucked in one day; and by the saw gin, 336 pounds[40].

The fibres emerging from the gin are called *lint*. Any fibrous fragments still attached to the seed, although useless for yarn, are not wasted. They are removed as *linters*, by a further gin, and used among other things for the production of artificial silk by the regenerated cellulose process.

In cotton, as in linen, the process of mechanization at first combined increase in speed with decrease in quality, compared with the hand-spinning of India. There was at that time a rich market for superlative textiles. There was also a plentiful supply of sweated labour, working long hours for little pay, so that the vast amount of time (years or even decades) required for the entire processes of spinning, weaving (cotton) or lace-making (linen) were not for the merchants a very serious consideration. It was only after two centuries of industrial revolution, democratization and spiralling wages that labour costs, and therefore hours of work (time consumed), became the prime and often the limiting factor in determining the quality of thread and lace that manufacturers could profitably produce. Lace was business: no profit, no production.

In India, at the time when the fabulous Dacca muslins were filling western hearts with covetousness, the fibres from the cotton tree were spun by the slenderest of spindles, stabilized by a tiny pellet of clay and supported on a shell so that its weight, slight as it was, could not tear apart the frail wisp of filament emerging miraculously from the sensitive movements of the spinner's hands. In the seventeenth century these hand-spun cotton singles were so fine that one pound of the raw material could be spun into 250 miles of yarn which could then be woven to make 73 yards of 36 inch wide muslin. For comparison, an English no. 350 cotton gives 167 miles.

Individually the fibres are immensely strong, their tensile strength being double that of wrought iron[41], but as a yarn cotton is much more delicate, since the short staples are held together only the spinner's skill, aided by their own constantly reversing surface convolutions. 'The strength of yarn is almost entirely dependent on the hold which the individual fibres take upon one another. Yarn does not break through the rupture of hairs, but through slip of hair on hair'[42]. In this respect, the maximum holding-together power is exerted by fibres with 150 to 175 half-convolutions to the inch, as in present-day Indian cotton. The Sea Island variety had 300, and this disadvantage as well as a lack of robustness in the plant itself, and its relatively low yield, made its yarn very expensive.

Although it appears that some cotton thread was produced in Venice in the thirteenth and fourteenth centuries, the hand-spinning of cotton was not easy for people accustomed to the longer and more sympathetic fibres of wool and flax. Neither the Great wheel (wool) nor the Saxony wheel (flax) adapted well to cotton, though the former could be used. The convolutions meant that once the twist was made the fibres were locked in position, and could not be drawn out further, so that the timing of drawing out and twisting had to be extremely sensitively judged. If too long a time was allowed, the short fibres would separate completely from each other, severing the yarn. If the time was too brief, they could be fixed immovably before they were sufficiently attenuated, resulting in lumpy areas along the yarn length, making it not only unsightly but quite unsuitable for lacemaking where threads need to be pulled smoothly, all the time, one against another.

The formation of the English East India Company in 1600 opened the way for the preferential importations of large quantities of raw cotton. Between 1700 and 1736, cotton fabrics were prohibited, but nor effectively prevented, from entering England, in order to avoid competition with the wool trade.

Then, with the invention of the Flying Shuttle and more rapid weaving in 1733, more thread was needed, and so the whole lumbering escapade of industrialization was set in motion with, as the decades passed, speed becoming far more important than personal skill, and the engineer taking over from the craftsman. A whole series of machines appeared in rapid succession: Hargreaves Spinning Jenny, developed between 1764 and 1770; Arkwright's Water Frame, 1769, the yarn from which was 'defective in fineness and tenuity'; Crompton's Mule, a cross between the longer draw of the Jenny and the greater firmness of the Water Frame, patented in 1779 though developed five years earlier; the Throstle Frame, c1800, which was a variation of the Water Frame, producing the smooth wiry 'water twist'; Robert's Self-acting Mule, first patented in 1825 and improved in 1830, which could spin soft downy 'mule yarn' in any count from 1s to upwards of 350s; and the Ring Spinning Frame, about 1832, which twisted the thread hard and firm but was suitable only for low counts. Together they transformed the cotton trade from a strong dependence on importations of fabric mainly from India, to importations of raw cotton, mainly from the West Indies and the USA, which could rapidly and with increasing efficiency be converted into thread.

Machine spinning, whatever its precise method, still incorporates the three basic movements of the hand spinner: that of drawing out and twisting the rovings, and of winding up the yarn so produced. In the Mule the process is *intermittent*, the two movements alternating with each other, as in the early hand wheel. In the Throstle (sometimes called the Flyer), and the Ring Spinner, the process is *continuous*, twisting and winding being carried on at the same time.

As in the case of flax, cotton fibres saturated with water are some 20% stronger than when they are dry. It follows that, especially for fine yarns, a controlled atmosphere of high humidity is essential.

Since the convolutions on the surface of the cotton fibres frequently change direction, from S to Z, they can in theory be spun in either direction with equal success. Peruvian cotton fabrics of 2500 BC are made of Z-spun singles doubled S. This twist causes the opposite spin of the singles to unwind until their fibres lie almost straight, and only the final S is at all clearly visible. For cotton, this reversal in plying makes a stronger thread since whichever way the fibres spiral with intake or loss of water, their movements must strengthen either the twist, or the ply. The ancient cotton fabrics of the Indus valley were woven from Z-spun singles, and there does appear to be some not-yet-understood advantage in this practise, since archeologists have found that while Z-spun fabrics wash well, S-spun fabrics tend to fall apart[43]. The complexities of S and Z spun yarns in relation to laces will be discussed in chapter 8.

However tightly the short staples of cotton are spun, the fibres are never entirely constrained. Any friction is likely to release some of the tips from their bondage, and they spring out from the thread, producing a fluffy appearance (fig. 35). This fluffiness

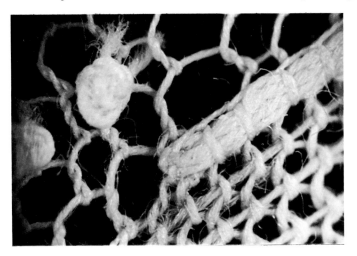

35. Brussels point de gaze, late 19th century. The cotton threads give a whiskery appearance under magnification.

is a disadvantage in lace, since ideally the design and perhaps even more importantly the multitudinously varied and often very beautiful thread movements which produce the decorative stitches need to be sharply clear or their whole impact is obscured. A means of removing the fluff by singeing it away in a gas flame was patented in 1817 by Samuel Hall, and so successfully that by 1821 he was making £25,000 to £30,000 a year out of the process[44]. Beneficial side effects of the singeing were that it raised the count of the yarn by reducing its weight, and improved the lustre of mercerized cotton by removing the cloudiness. There was a slight strengthening but, less desirably, a darkening of the colour[45].

**Mercerized cotton**, marketed by Coats as 'Sylko', is prepared and spun in exactly the same way as ordinary cotton yarn, then subjected to treatment with sodium hydroxide solution varying in strength from 15 to 30%. That is, the mercerization process comes after normal spinning.

### Silk

The cultivation of silk is an intensive process but, as an externally occurring filament-fibre, silk is not only all in one piece – for 1,000 yards at least – but it needs no excavation to uncover it. Thus it escapes many of the problems which beset the preparation of flax and cotton yarns, most notably perhaps the problem of getting the fibre ultimates (individual cells) to stay together, and to cling lengthwise to one another to make a smooth, adequately strong thread out of small separate particles. While linen, cotton and wool all begin with a mass which then has to be thinned by separation, silk begins with single fibres which have to be thickened by grouping them together.

The reeling of silk from the cocoons has already been described. In spite of mechanization this stage is still best done by hand because of the ability of the human reelers to sense the ends of the fibres as they narrow, and to judge the precise moment for splicing on the new cocoons using the worm's own seracin.

Since spinning in its full sense is not necessary (there is no drawing out, or drafting), the raw silk is simply degummed and then *thrown*, i.e. twisted together with other filaments to make a thicker yarn. The twists may be either S or Z, and their number per unit length may vary. Sometimes two or three untwisted singles are doubled, and twisted 70 or 75 turns to right or left. With all the possibilities of direction of twist, number of filaments per single, number of twists per single, and the number and tightness of the twists in doubling, a wide range of silk threads for different purposes can be produced.

**Spun silk** is made of fragments of silk waste and broken filaments which cannot be reeled or thrown. It is spun in a manner similar to that for linen. The Mule can be used.

### Wool

The staple fibres of wool are crinkly and scaly and have a natural tendency to cling together to the extent of becoming tangled, matted or even felted. Like cotton and silk they occur as single fibres, externally, and so have none of the laborious problems of extraction and separation which are the essential preliminaries to the spinning of flax. Nor do they have cotton's problem of the tenacious seeds, or silk's problem of care for the worms followed by treatment and preservation of the cocoons. Wool fibres need only to be cut off, or plucked, or combed from the living sheep, cleansed, straightened and drawn past one another to produce a controlled quantity of fibres which can be twisted together in a consistent manner to form a yarn. The ease of drawing out determines the thickness or thinness that can be achieved during spinning. Fibres with large scales catch on each other, clinging together in a coarse strand. The smaller the scales, the more easily the fibres glide, and the finer the yarns that can be made from them.

If wool has a problem it is that the fibres' helpful qualities have a less favourable aspect. The scaliness for example, which helps them to cling together during spinning, can if carried to excess cause them to become knotted into tangles; while the crinkles which give them a springy quality and a natural elasticity, and make them easy to spin since the 'waves' of neighbouring aligned fibres lock into each other, may less advantageously make it difficult to control the size of the end-product.

Both spinning and the process of lacemaking involve stretching the fibres, pulling them sufficiently tightly to make a yarn or fabric of even tension. But when wool has an opportunity to relax it will do so. Even taking it off the bobbin lace-pillow, where it is fixed by pins, may result in a 30% reduction in size – a formidable effect, that may be counteracted by making the lace that much bigger in the first place. Washing, however gentle, involves the addition of moisture, and the reversion of the molecules to their folded state in which they occupy less space, i.e. the threads become shorter and thicker, in effect they shrink.

The fibres of the fleece are pulled repeatedly against fine wire hooks to separate and straighten them until they lie parallel to each other. This is *carding*. The loosely twisted roll of wool which results is called a *rolag*. It corresponds to the rove of flax or cotton. It can be used directly for hand-spinning, the fibres being drawn out and twisted as the spindle rotates. When they are scaly enough and crinkly enough to hold together easily, a drop-spindle can be used so that it hangs free, allowing the spinner to stand and walk about, as nomadic people must certainly have done, or village women and children minding the flocks of sheep as they grazed.

Wool can be spun equally well in an S or a Z direction. In Egypt, with its long tradition of linen spinning, an S-spin was most common, while in India with its vast experience of cotton, the Z spin was preferred. There seems no difference in the quality of the final products. In surviving fragments from the Bronze Age in northern Europe, S-spun singles spiralled around each other in a Z direction appear to have predominated between 1800 and 1000 BC. After that, S plyed S occurs more frequently[46].

The tightness of the spin depends on the end-use or sink to which the thread is directed. The fewer the turns, the softer the yarn, so that a low twist would be suitable for lacy knitted shawls (fig. 36 colour), and a higher twist for the stout bobbin laces known as Yak and Cluny (see fig. 23b).

Various types of spinning wheel can be used, such as the Great wheel, and others similar to the Flax wheel (Brunswick or Saxon wheel). When the flyer and bobbin are rotated clockwise, a Z-spin will be produced in the yarn. The spinner's fingers no longer need to turn the fibres, only to draft them, and the longer she holds the rotating draw before allowing the yarn to wind on, the more turns will be inserted, making a harder yarn. The required texture is not calculated but felt, and can be adapted with great flexibility to the intended sink. Commercially wool is spun mainly on machines similar to the Mules used for cotton, and counts of 125 can be obtained[47].

Goats' wool may well have been spun, using a hand-held spindle, before that of sheep was attempted. Having fewer scales – the Cashmere goat has only 6 to 8 per 100 microns length[48] – the hairs could be separated by beating, and would draw out more readily into strands straight enough for spinning. The rough shaggy coverings of primitive sheep on the other hand, with their larger and more numerous scales, would be less easy to spin but could be compacted into felt, and so would form a usable fabric without the labour of weaving.

Wool or worsted yarns are often doubled, or plyed, to make them stronger. In plying on the wheel, twin bobbins of yarn take, in effect, the place of the rolag. They are turned as for spinning, but most often with the wheel rotated anti-clockwise so that two Zs are plyed with an S twist. Singles, too tightly twisted, will coil up and spiral around each other, in the reverse direction, thus slackening the original spin, and perhaps improving the lustre. Plying in the same direction (S plyed S or Z plyed Z) not only reinforces the twist, making a harder thread, but also causes the fibres to become more and more stretched from a vertical to a near hori-zontal direction, scattering the light and producing a dull appearance.

***Man-made fibres***

**(a) Regenerated cellulose**. In essence, the method of manufacture of artificial silk mimics the actions of the silkworm. Just as the worm eats mulberry leaves and converts their substance into the protein fibroin, so Chardonnet, starting with the cellulose of cotton linters, dissolved and then extruded them through spinnerets, allowing the narrow filaments to harden on exposure to air. Subsequently he reconverted the yarn into pure cellulose. In spite of the difference in their chemical composition – the man-made being cellulose while the insect's are protein – the resultant filaments, whether cuprammonium, viscose or acetate, have remarkable similarities to natural silk in their smooth slender length and glossy lustre. They have the further advantage that, by varying the size of the 'spinnerets', they can be made to any length or width desired by the manufacturer, and therefore the normal need for singles and doubles does not so strongly apply. Acetate differs from the other two in remaining as cellulose acetate without being reconverted, and for this reason it was not included under the trade name *rayon* when this was adopted in 1924 (fig. 37a,b).

**(b) Regenerated proteins, alginates and synthetics** are all extruded in a similar manner, forming smooth fibres of almost infinite length. There are now a vast number of synthetic fibre variations within the three main groups of polyamides, polyesters and acrylics. Staple forms can also be manufactured and spun like cotton, for example *spun polyester*.

## Minerals

The metals gold, silver and copper are not of course fibres at all. Sheets of metal are beaten to a thin foil (gold can be reduced to 1/280,000th inch in thickness), cut into strips about 0.5mm wide, then neatly curled in a spiral manner around a core of silk or cotton strands, of matching colour, to make a fairly pliable thread (fig. 38, colour). One grain of gold (1/5,760th of one pound Troy weight, or 12 ounces) can be beaten until it covers 56 square feet, or it can be drawn out until it forms a wire 500 foot long, comparable in diameter to the filaments of silk or synthetic fibres[49].

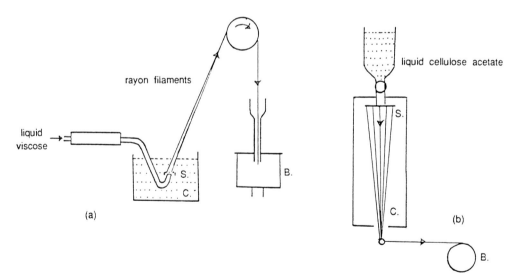

37a. Viscose rayon fibres congealed in liquid (C = coagulating bath).

b. Cellulose acetate fibres solidified in air (C = hot air chamber). (Both after A.J.Hall).

S = spinneret; B = bobbin for winding on filaments.

# 7 *Which thread is it?*

The threads used in different laces may sometimes help to identify them. For example, if a lace is made of cotton, it will date from after 1800 or, if hand-made, from after 1815 or more likely 1830. Linen yarn was little used for fashion laces after 1850, though it continues to be used for peasant laces up to modern times. Nineteenth-century machine laces were not made of linen, which snapped too easily under pressure. In the twentieth century, coarser dry-spun linen is sometimes used on the Barmen machine for torchon designs. Silk laces are mainly restricted to countries where silkworm culture can be practised economically, for example north Italy, France, Spain, Malta and Russia or, after 1900, China.

Modern techniques for fibre identification are complex, sophisticated, laborious and extremely accurate. They have great value in the analysis of archeological finds, where an evolution of fibre usage can be established.

As far as lace is concerned, however, there was little need for scientific distinctions to be drawn before the nineteenth century when cotton's appearance on the scene, as an inexpensive flax substitute, opened the door to all kinds of fraudulent practises, cotton being passed off not only as the more expensive linen in contemporary productions, but also being used – because around 1900 its superfine thread excelled that of linen – to reconstruct antique laces which dishonest or misguided dealers might then pass off as two centuries older than in fact they were.

In the seventeenth century, Pepys had listened in to a discussion about the import duty to be levied on cotton fabrics. In the nineteenth century the urgency related to lace, and a report of the 1842 Paris Exhibition contained the following passage, quoted by Mme Despierres:

'Thanks to the intelligent research of M. Clerget, employed at the Customs Office, it is possible today to identify with certainty cotton thread. Under a micro-scope, magnifying 300 times, cotton threads present the exact appearance of a narrow ribbon: linen on the other hand divides out into smooth filaments marked at intervals by crossed lines, rather like knotted reeds'.

In 1878, a chemical method of distinguishing the fibres was described: soak both in a solution of sugar and salt (sodium chloride), allow the fibres or yarn to dry, then set fire to them. The linen threads are carbonized with a grey colour, the cotton takes on black.

Laundrywomen had their own tests: when linen was washed it had a light cream tint, while cotton immediately became very white.[50]

Many of the fibre aspects and features summarized in tables 2 and 3, can serve as diagnostic pointers for identification. But there are other quite special tests, some just as unrepeatable by the unequipped layman as were the moisture regain, specific gravity, elongation to break and so forth, already referred to.

Even more enlightening tests, such as carbon-14 dating with its plus or minus factor of 100 years, probably have little relevance over the 400-year period of lace in fashion. Also, much depends on the treatment to which the lace has been subjected in wear, wash and storage. The degree of polymerization, though significant for prognosis of the fibre's future life expectancy, gives little information about its past since depolymerization can be brought about by so many different factors.

A word of warning: some of the tests require expensive equipment, and others the use of potentially dangerous chemicals. However, for the general collector or lacemaker or student interested practically rather than passionately in identification, the visual and tactile qualities of the thread, plus a ×80 magnification, are likely to be sufficient. It is a question of substituting probabilities for the maximum possible certainty.

Oversimplification can of course prove a dangerous boomerang, giving misleading results and inaccurate conclusions. So, for those needing, or having the facilities for, greater accurancy, further details of the basic test-possibilities can be found in The Textile Institute's *Identification of Textile Materials*.

Another and not easily surmountable problem is that most of the tests depend on some threads of the lace being freely available. When antique laces are in perfect condition, with not a loose end anywhere in sight, then staining, burning and indeed nearly everything other than superficial or microscopic examination are impossible, and even obtaining a detailed assessment of the diameter of randomized fibres, the number of fibres present in the yarn, the width of the yarn, or the number of twists per unit length, involves considerable problems and necessitates extremely cautious handling when an entire piece of lace has to be manoeuvred beneath the objective. Additionally, the more rarely used stem and leaf fibres can be accurately identified only

when other tissues are also present, and they will not be, in lace.

For unmade-up threads, intended for lacemaking but never used, rendered anonymous by the loss of labels, and perhaps already well over 100 years old, all the tests are much easier to carry out.

If you intend to experiment, try your hand first with modern threads which are replaceable, not with antique laces which are not.

It should be noted that considerable differences exist between the genetic varieties of flax and of cotton plants. The fibres of Belgian flax for example are a good deal longer than those of Ireland[51]. Similar differences exist between genetic varieties of sheep, so that broad generalizations are difficult to make with accuracy and the information given in table 4 is intended for guidance rather than as a dogmatic statement.

39b to f. Cross-sections of fibres investigated in Table4.
b. linen. c. cotton (courtesy B.T.T.G.).
(cont. p.47).

b

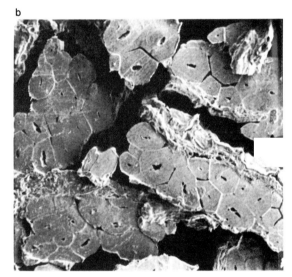

c

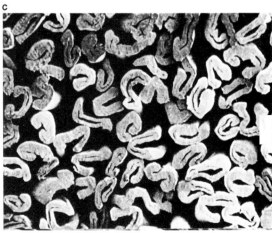

39a. Detail of a Burano lace imitating a 17th-century Venetian needle lace. Made in cotton. Note the flattened effect produced by an aficot.

**Table 4**  FIBRE AND THREAD IDENTIFICATION TESTS

Note: L = linen; C = cotton; S = silk; W = wool; R = regenerated; SY = synthetic.

**Superficial observation**

<u>Visual</u>  a.  Clear versus cloudy. The long fibres of flax, and the filaments of silk, rayon and synthetics, produce a sharp outline with no irregularities of shape, colour or texture to detract from the clarity of the lace's design or the lucidity of its technique. Shorter staples such as cotton and wool, linen tow, and the spun forms of silk, rayons and synthetics cannot, even with tighter twisting, control their more frequent ends so firmly and the tips spring out from the yarn during lacemaking, and even more with use, to produce a fabric which, at least under magnification, appears decidedly hairy.

b.  Lustre. The lustre or sheen of a fibre is a measure of the amount of light it reflects, and this is directly related to the smoothness of its outer surface which concentrates the reflected light into bright uni-directional beams. Any irregularity tends to break up and scatter that light, so the greater the size of the scales (wool) or the depth of convolutions (cotton), the more the light is dispersed, producing a matt appearance. The spin, by smoothing the surface irregularities of the fibres into a more perfect cylinder of yarn, can increase the lustre. However as the spin becomes harder, so the diversion of the fibres from the straight to something approaching horizontal scatters the reflected light and the thread becomes dull. The natural glossy sheen of linen, resulting from the wax on the fibre surface, is increased by the removal of the gum binding the fibres together, and it can be further augmented by rubbing the lace with a smooth implement - an aficot, a rounded glass weight, or a lobster's claw - which crushes and smooths the fibres, distributing the wax as a continuous covering layer. The pale golden glow of silk - enriched by the removal of sericin - combined with the gliding motion of its filaments, give it a richness of aspect completely in tune with its extravagant cost. Since the fibres are very smooth, the best yarn lustre is obtained by a soft spin which allows the filaments to lie almost straight. The excessive brilliance of synthetics can be toned down by delustering with titanium dioxide.

c.  The visible spin. All the main fibres can be spun in either direction, S or Z, though with a particular fibre one or other direction may produce a more satisfactory yarn. Spin and ply therefore have no great diagnostic value in identification, but they do affect the lace, and should be noted.

d.  Fibre joinings. Natural filament fibres may sometimes be distinguished from synthetics by the presence of joins, either knotted or spliced, in the lace. Knots may help to identify relatively short filaments such as horsehair, with a maximum length of some eight-and-a-half feet. Artificial horsehair is as long as the manufacturer wishes to make it - except that both bobbin and needle lace techniques require lengths short enough to be manageable with a sewing needle, or to wind onto the necks of bobbins, so that laces handmade from synthetic yarn would still show joins, though at different intervals. However, artificial horsehair laces made on the Barmen machine will be knotless since the large spools hold very considerable quantities of thread. Natural silk is not easy to distinguish, visually, from artificial. See <u>Chemical tests:</u> silk is protein, artificial silk is cellulose.

e.  Drying behaviour. If flax fibres are dampened by pulling them between wettened fingers, then held vertically and the free tips observed from above, they will be seen to rotate in a clockwise direction as they dry. The fibres of ramie and nettle behave in the same way, and must be distinguished by other means. Hemp, and most other bast fibres, rotate in the reverse (anti-clockwise) direction. Cotton fibres twist first in one direction and then the other, driven by their alternating convolutions.

<u>Tactile</u>  a.  Light versus heavy. Density, hardness of spin, thickness of yarn, and the size and solidity of the design areas all affect the feel of the lace. The pleasingly supple weight of linen laces which, however aerily light their construction, still appear to press coolly upon the hand when lifted, results additionally from a combination of thick fibre walls, the presence of a minute amount of lignin (wood), and the compact fitting together of the fibres within the yarn. The central column of air inside cotton fibres and, in wool, the presence of air between fibres held apart by their scales and crenellations, make both seem light for their bulk.

b.  Temperature. The warm or cold feel of a lace depends largely, as with other objects, on the speed with which it conducts heat away from the touching hand. However, enclosed air, acting as an insulator, makes wool and cotton warmer than is justified by their quite good thermal conductivity. See *Table 3*.

c.  Cotton versus linen. Hold the yarn tightly between the finger tips, then pull it through. Linen will emerge stiff and straight, cotton will be limp and drooping through loss of air.

-----------------------------------------------------------------------------------------------------------------------------

**Microscopic observation**

a.     Fibre shape:

(i) Cross section (figs.39 b-f):

L. Irregular in size and shape, but approximately hexagonal with walls so thick there is almost no central cavity, and it is heavy and cold to the touch. Thinner walls denote poor quality, but the thickness should be cellulose: increased amounts of lignin, in older plants, make the fibres hard.

C. Like a collapsed tube irregularly curved. The shape will depend on which part of the twist the section goes through. The fibres are thin-walled and the central cavity is filled with air.

S. Rounded triangles, initially cemented together in pairs by sericin. In wild silks, the shape is slightly different.

W. Round, but coarse scales make it look slightly rough on theoutside.

R. Viscose rayon is crenellated, but other regenerated cellulose fibres may be round, flattened or folded.

S. The shape depends on the spinnerets used, and is controlled by the manufacturer. They are normally round, trilobal or tetralobal, but may be bicomponent (see fig.60).

(ii) Lengthwise, surface features:

L. Bamboo-like, with pronounced nodes. The fairly short ultimates may taper at the ends.

C. Ribbon-like with convolutions which change direction. The number of these spirals per inch varies with the variety, for example Sea Island 300, Egyptian 228, Brazilian 210, American 192, Indian 150.

S. Smooth surface, very long.

W. Surface scales and a central core or medulla. The size of the scales and their number per unit length vary with the type of wool. In general, the finer fibres such as merino and cashmere have a greater number of, and more regular, scales each completely encircling the hair. Merino for example, able to produce wools of 80s quality, has the highest number, 2000 per inch length, with cashmere almost as many. The number of crimps per inch also varies (see p.20). Viscose rayon: longitudinal striations or ridges.

SY. Smooth surface.

b.     Fibre dimensions:     Lengths are given in _Table 2_.
                                        Widths:

L.  11 to 31 microns.

C.  The finest is Sea Island cotton (11.5 to 13 microns), the coarsest Madras and Nankin (14.5 to 22 microns).

S.  9 to 11 microns.

W.  Fine 18 to 27 microns (Merino) up to 40 microns (coarse). Cashmere measures 13 microns.

R.  12 to 100 microns, according to manufacture.

SY.  12 microns upwards, in decreasing fineness. Varied by the manufacturer.

c.     Crystals: Different crystal forms can be discovered in the ash from many fibres, but high magnification is required to see them.

d.     Birefringence: expresses the difference between the refractive index measured widthwise and lengthwise of the fibre (refractive index = the bending of the light rays as they pass from one substance to another eg from the fibre to the air or surrounding liquid). Birefringencies can be determined only by using a polarising microscope, which is rather costly but gives an entrancing range of vividly distinctive colours - green, orange, yellow, turquoise and magenta - of almost fluorescent brilliance. Examples of measurements are : Linen .06, Cotton .048, Silk .053, Wool .01, Viscose .022, Acetate .003, Nylon (6.6) .056, Acrylic -.003, Polyester .16   (Textile Institute).

-----------------------------------------------------------------------------------------------------------------------------------

**Burning**

Cellulose fibres ignite rapidly with a yellow flame, giving a smell of burning paper. They continue to burn when the flame is removed, leaving a little feathery grey ash, without crystals. cellulose acetate (regenerated cellulose) melts then flares quickly, smelling like vinegar (acetic acid), and leaving a black crunchy ash.

Proteins smoulder slowly with an odour of burning hair. The small flame splutters and sizzles, leaving a crisp dark knob which is easily crushed.

Nylon melts and burns slowly, tending to go out when the flame is removed. It smells something like celery and the residue is a tough grey bead.

-----------------------------------------------------------------------------------------------------------------------------------

**Chemical tests** including solubility and staining:

a. Alkalis. Strong (5%) caustic soda dissolves wool and silk but not flax or cotton. Cotton remains white, but linen turns yellowish. In 2% caustic soda, calcium alginate turns bright yellow.

b. Dilute (2%) sulphuric acid will char a cellulose thread. Place the acidified thread between blotting paper and press with a hot iron. Animal fibres are not affected.

c. With concentrated sulphuric acid followed by weak ammonia, cotton dissolves, linen is unaffected.

d. Concentrated cold hydrochloric acid dissolves silk and causes wool to swell. Hydrochloric acid also dissolves nylon.

e. Sodium hypochlorite (with 5% available chlorine) is an oxidising agent which dissolves silk. It was used in early 'chemical laces' to disintegrate the backing fabric onto which a cotton design was embroidered by the Schiffli machine. Cotton is damaged by chlorine bleaches at high temperatures.

f. Stain: 9% fuschin in alcohol produces a rose-red colour in cotton and linen. If ammonia is then added, linen keeps its colour, cotton loses it.

g. With zinc-chlor-iodide (Herzberg's stain, a test for cellulose), linen becomes a bluish-purple colour, cotton a reddish-purple, and mercerised cotton a very dark purple, almost black.

h. A 50:50 solution of concentrated sulphuric acid and iodine crystals distinguishes the regenerated celluloses: viscose turns dark blue, cuprammonium light blue and acetate yellow.

i. Millon's reagent (a test for protein) causes animal fibres to turn pink or red; plant fibres are unaffected.

j. Aniline sulphate (a test for lignin) stains flax slightly yellow and pineapple fibres colourless to yellow. It has no effect on cotton, silk, wool, rayons or synthetics.

K. Phloroglucinol with hydrochloric acid (a test for lignin) stains linen very slightly red, and pineapple colourless to light red.

l. Cellulose acetate is the only fibre which dissolves in acetone.

m. Old and new cotton fibres can be distinguished by ultra-violet light: the new show a violet fluorescence, the old an ivory to brownish-white tinge.

There are numerous other chemical tests for distinguishing fibres. Details can be found in *The Identification of Textile Materials*.

Identification of the many varieties of synthetic fibres is not particularly relevant to lace since they are all very young and give no assistance to the recognition of antique forms. They are distinguished by tests such as density, melting point, refractive index, birefringency, use of X-ray diffraction units, infrared spectrometers, chromatographs, and electron microscopes.

There are also specialised tests for distinguishing different bast and leaf fibres; silk and tussah etc. These again are superfluous to the aims of this book.

39d. silk

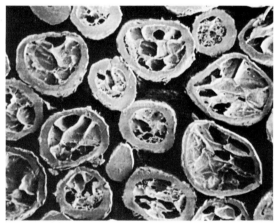

39e. wool

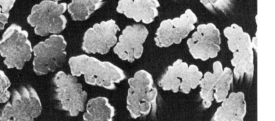

39f. viscose rayon
(all courtesy: B.T.T.G.).

40. A bobbin lace: the various parts. a. solid design areas made of (i) clothstitch, (ii) halfstitch; b. openwork ground, here of Mechlin type; c. decorative stitches; d. heading.

41. Ways of moving threads to make laces (openwork techniques): see pp.49-51

# 8 Threads make lace

The various organic, historical, chemical and physical origins or *sources* of lace threads have now been examined, and it is time to consider how they are applied to their end-uses, or *sinks*. In other words, to consider how threads make lace.

The method used for the conversion is called the *technique*. Single or multiple threads are moved in a strictly defined manner to make the 'slender open-work fabrics' which we know as lace.

As we have seen, lacemakers did not invent the threads they used, but adopted those which early civilizations had long since selected. Lace techniques, similarly, were based on much more ancient forms of thread movement.

The only true originality added by lace was open-work, not just the idea of it which was already well-known, but the emphasis on it as the very essence of lace creation, whether the holes related primarily to the background areas or to the design (fig. 40). Addi-

tionally, the fabric became decorative rather than functional. In this way, practical knotting, used for nets or snares, developed into laces such as filet, or the gaily coloured silk needle-knotted laces of the Middle East. Knotting of groups of threads as opposed to single ones turned into the simple warp-knotted fringes of South America and the more elaborate ornamental knotting known as macramé. The twisting technique of sprang, found in Egyptian tombs and in Bronze Age Denmark as nets for encapsulating the hair, has developmental similarities to those important bobbin laces made by intertwining threads around each other in a vertical direction. The looping, originally intended for continuous fabrics, became diversified into fine laces made with a needle or hook, such as needlepoint, knitting and crochet. Lace machines readily adapted knitting and twisting to their own purposes (figs. 41a–g, b and f in colour).

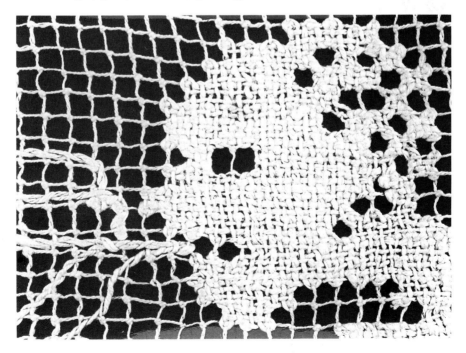

41a. filet
(photo: John Knight,
courtesy
W.S.C.A.D.)

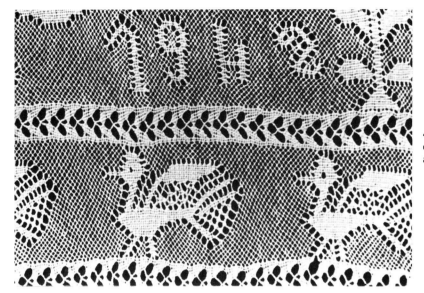

41c. a shawl from Ecuador, the warp
ends knotted with half-hitches,
a form of macrame

Not until the sixteenth century was a firm bond established between lace and commerce. Then, two techniques rapidly transcended all others in economic importance, one using the looping movement developed in the Stone Age; the other the twining technique reminiscent of sprang or the plaiting of warp ends in a woven cloth. The first technique became known as *needle* or *needlepoint* lace; the second as *bobbin*, *pillow* or *bone* lace.

41d. macrame

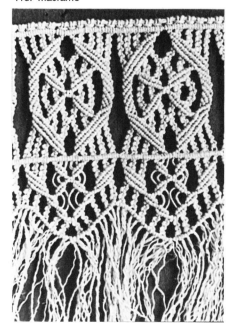

## Turning threads into lace

**1. Openwork embroidery**, a method of turning a solid woven fabric into a holey one. In *drawnwork*, threads of warp and/or weft may be removed in whole or in part, and the residual strands bound around to create a series of tiny openwork squares. Or, where the weave is sufficiently loose, threads are not removed but simply pulled tightly together in intricate arrangements which involve constant thread-counting and decorative needle-manipulations to create a vast and beautiful variety of effects. These two techniques, frequently referred to as 'drawn' and 'pulled' threadwork, are characteristic of different geographical areas (figs. 42a,b).

**2. Cutwork** is an extension of drawnwork, the removal of small groups of warps and wefts being superseded by the cutting out of entire blocks of fabric to leave squares which are then partially infilled with geometric patterns. In these pattern areas are resurrected the loops or 'needle-binding' of prehistoric times (fig. 43a, colour).

**3. Reticella.** The cut-outs of the previous technique were initially of variable shape. Soon they became square, and the decorations within them extremely elaborate and time-consuming. Merchants, with an eye to profit, discovered that time and money could be saved by substituting frames ready-made, by plaiting or needle-weaving, for the laborious cutting away of laboriously woven cloth which the cutwork technique itself entailed (fig. 43b).

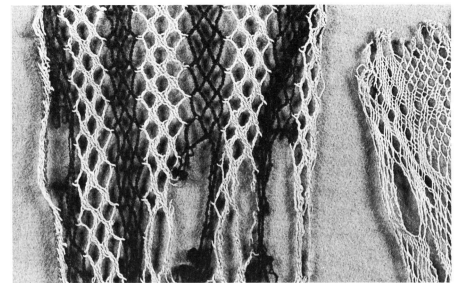

41e. sprang, Upper Egypt,
4th to 5th century AD
(courtesy V and A)

41g.  lace made on the Leavers machine.

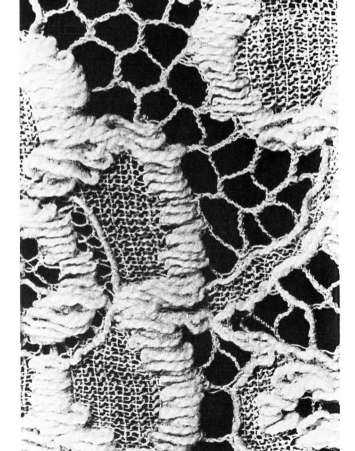

(For 41b and f see colour pages)

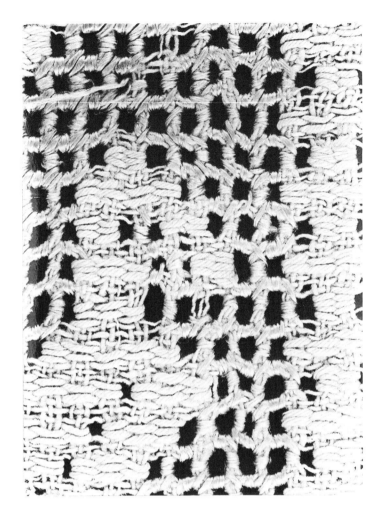

42a.  Russian drawnwork, 16th century.
Warps and wefts are drawn out,
without cutting, and the strengthened
meshes overdarned to make the design
(photo: John Knight, courtesy W.S.C.A.D.).

42b. Pulled threadwork. The entire
background, as well as the
decorative stitches, are made by
counting the threads and pulling them
together in prearranged groups.
None are taken out.  English,
18th century.

## 4. Needle laces.

Reticella was the parent of needle laces. Its two essential features, the laying down of a frame or outline within which the work was constructed, and the use of looping movements to produce the stitches, are found in all needle laces wherever or whenever they have been made. The basic loop and loop-and-twist stitches (figs. 43c,d) have, in them, become refined into the many variations of the so-called detached buttonhole stitch which became, during the eighteenth century, so transcendently minute that 10,000 of them could be accommodated within one square inch (fig. 43e).

43 b. Reticella c1600 - the horizontal supports are plaited, the vertical needlewoven, the diagonal corded; c. Loop stitch; d(i). Loop and twist (Hald, p.127). Both c and d(i) are worked spirally so that the stitches are the same all the time. Arrows indicate the direction of working. d(ii). Loop and twist with a straight return used as a decorative stitch in mid-19th century Alencon lace. Note the variable thickness of the S-plyed-S linen thread.

(43.a. see colour pages)

d(ii)

c

d(i)

53

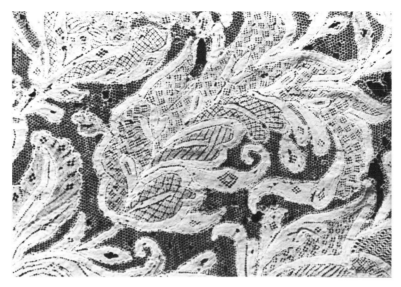

43.e. Reseau Venise

(43.f. see colour pages)

43.g. *Yucca* plant, showing the sharply pointed leaf tips that can be used as needles.

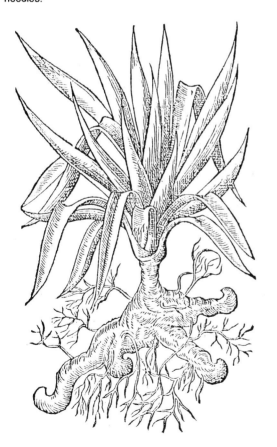

In prehistoric objects such as strainers, socks, bags and baskets (fig. 43f, colour), short lengths of thread made of Z-twined hairs from a cow's tail, or from wool, cotton, agave or chewed bark, were worked in a looping movement and a spiral sequence using either human fingers, primitive needles made from sharp spines such as the leaf tips of yucca (fig. 43g), or proper wood, bronze or bone needles with eyes[52]. This technique appeared worldwide, and both ancient and modern objects are known from Arizona, Africa, Indonesia, Mexico, Peru, and the whole north-eastern half of Australia.

In the needle laces of the sixteenth and later centuries, the thread was transcendentally sumptuous linen, its development linked with that of the Brunswick wheel, around 1530, which could spin better, finer and faster than was possible before. The implements were minute wire needles of toughened steel, first introduced into Europe by the Moors, and in production at Nuremberg by 1370. The lacemaking areas were all within Europe until the nineteenth century when, for the tourist trade, centres sprang up wherever visitors could be persuaded to purchase.

There was a further and very important distinction. The prehistoric technique was three-dimensional and spiral, the lace technique two-dimensional and horizontal (fig. 44). This difference profoundly affects the relationship of thread movements to thread spin.

When the square-framed reticella form was abandoned in favour of more flowing shapes, the laces were referred to as 'stitches in the air' or *punto in aria*, the term indicating the lack of any base fabric

54

in which the stitches could be embedded. They were made quite literally in the air, above the pattern. Splendidly sophisticated laces of this type were by the later sixteenth century the darlings of all the royal courts of Europe, replacing almost at a stroke the preceding obsession with glittering passements of gaudy silk and gold made by a plaiting technique (figs. 45, 46). Neither silk (which slipped), nor precious metals (the edges of which caught against each other as they were drawn through the loops) could be used for needle laces, whereas linen thread which, by the second half of the sixteenth century, was being woven into exquisite lawns and cambrics, was ideal for the purpose. So began the long tradition, which was to last for the next 300 years, of linen as the thread from which all the best laces were made.

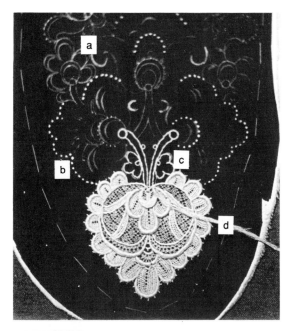

44(i). Making a needle lace. The threads which make the stitches encircle the cord supports at either end for additional security. a = drawn design; b = holes pricked for couching threads to pass through; c = foundation cord laid; d = padding strands for cordonnet.

(ii). An unusual construction: there are no stitches, an S-plyed cord has been twisted into free-standing teeth; or, a thick thread has been wound around a convoluted wire support. The ruff is edged with bobbin lace. *Portrait of a Young Lady with a Ruff*, Paulus Moreelse, detail (courtesy: The Carnegie Museum of Art, Pittsburgh, bequest of Howard A. Noble, 1964).

45. Punto in aria, 16th century designs.

46. Portrait of Christine Gravaus by Wolfgang
Heimbach, 1636, showing a splendid coif in cutwork, or
reticella (courtesy: Adbruck PostKarte).

**5. Weaving**, and the modifications of it to produce lace, involve not single threads as in (1) to (4), but many threads worked together.

(a) The earliest form may well have been **LOOM LACES**, a kind of gauze weave with extended areas of openwork produced by manipulation of the warps. They are known from Peru, 1000-1400 AD (cotton); south Italy, seventeenth century (linen or silk); and Denmark and Germany, nineteenth and twentieth centuries (linen) (fig. 47a,b). In some cases instead of the gauze being patterned on the loom, it was woven plain and called *buratto*, then embroidered with a running stitch, using brightly dyed floss silks on a coloured silk ground, or white linen on a white linen ground. A book, *Il Burato*, illustrating designs for this embroidery, was printed in Venice by Paganino in 1527 (figs. 48a,b).

56

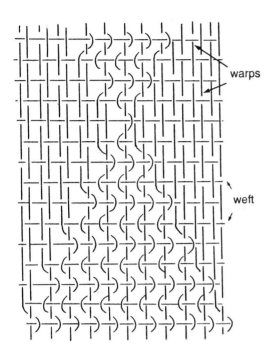

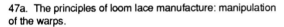

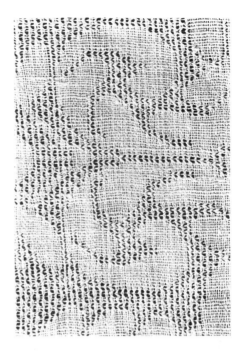

47a. The principles of loom lace manufacture: manipulation of the warps.

47b. A loom lace, linen, Germany or Denmark, 19th century.

48a. Detail of a linen buratto lace embroidered with a horse's head, 17th century (photo: John Knight, courtesy: W.S.C.A.D.).

48b. The title page of *Il Burato*, 1527 (courtesy: Cornell University).

(49.a. see colour pages)

49b. Binche, c1700: the rounded design is perfectly displayed by the delicate balance of solid and open areas, worked in a supremely fine linen thread.

49c. Point d'Angleterre, c1700. The raised work indicates a non-continuous-thread technique.

(b) **BOBBIN LACES** are so named because each thread is allocated a thread-holder or bobbin, around the neck of which it is wound, several yards at a time, in a consistent direction, being secured there by a half-hitch which is easily loosened to release short lengths as the lacemaker requires them. Figs. 49a (colour) and b–e, show a little of the immense variety of bobbin laces.

49d. Bucks point: a fan leaf worked in slender cotton, using the continuous thread technique (photo: John Knight, courtesy: W.S.C.A.D.).

49e. Bohemian bobbin lace, non-continuous-thread technique, with sewings (credit as d).

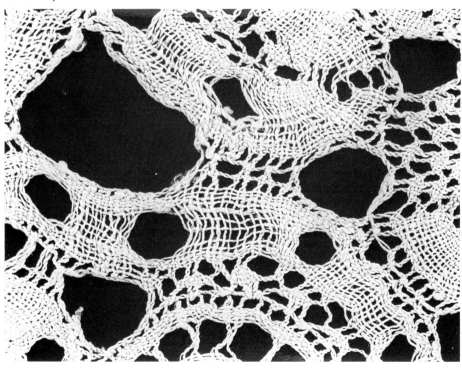

Lace was made by moving the bobbins in pairs, so that the threads passed over each other in either a left-to-right or a right-to-left direction. Yet out of this simplicity sprang an amazing wealth of intricate stitches and an almost infinite complexity of design (fig. 50).

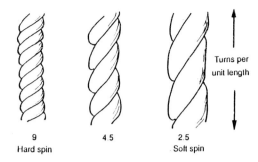

52.b. In general, the thicker the thread, the fewer the turns.

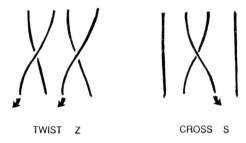

TWIST  Z                    CROSS  S

50. The two movements by which all bobbin laces are constructed.

### Interaction of lace and thread

On a simple level, for purely mechanical reasons such as rough edges (metal or wool) or slipperiness (silk) some fibres are unsuitable for needle laces. Wool, and metal coated with wax to facilitate its passings, can be used for bobbin laces, though not so easily as linen, cotton or silk (fig. 51, colour).

Much more deadly are the conflicts of tension which can arise between the movements of the yarn in lacemaking, and the twist of the yarn resulting from its spin. As Sonday has pointed out[53], cross, twist and loop each have their own S or Z formations (figs. 50, 52a), which must inevitably interact, agreeably or otherwise, with the S or Z spirals already present in the thread.

It is all a question of balance. At their original source, flax and cotton fibres lie straight. When they are artificially rotated into a spiral form, although the central fibres will be only lightly twisted, the outer must pass in increasing angles of stretch and stress around them. The degree of stress generated will be proportional to the tightness of the twist, and this can be expressed as the number of *turns per inch*, or t.p.i (fig. 52b). In the behaviour of the yarns during lacemaking, the turns per inch, or per millimetre, are at least as important as the *twist direction* since they affect the lustre, strength and elasticity of the thread, which the direction alone does not. In fact what will actually happen when either S or Z spun yarns are used for either S or Z directional yarn movements, will depend on whether the stress already suffered by the yarn can be increased or decreased without traumatic effect.

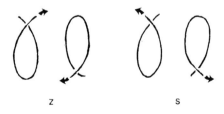

z                    s

52.a. As the loop is closed, the thread must cross over itself in either an S or a Z direction.

52.c. Auto-plying: this tendency makes the thread difficult to work with. (i) balanced, becomes (ii) unbalanced or snarled when too tightly spun. The S yarns ply themselves Z.

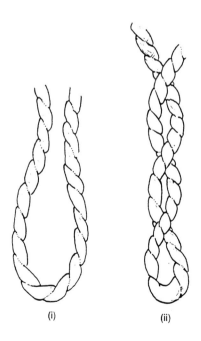

(i)                    (ii)

Since flax fibres rotate in an S direction as they dry, a yarn wet-spun in a Z direction will gradually unwind as water is lost, and there is a danger of the fibres straightening to the extent of losing their hold on each other. If however a Z-spin is followed by an S-ply, they will be locked safely together once more.

In fact, singles cannot be spun really tightly without snarling, since the tighter the twist the greater the tendency of the yarn to coil back on itself in the reverse direction, in effect to auto-ply (fig. 52c). Plying in a direction opposite to the original spin strengthens the thread and allows a harder twist to be inserted without ill effect. In a doubled thread, the strains of the component yarns can be *balanced* (see ch. 9), the outer twist unwinding the inner tension until the fibres can relax into an almost straight position. On the other hand, first and second spins in the same direction (S plyed S or Z plyed Z), though in theory they produce a harder stronger thread, may introduce elements of over-twisting, instability and weakness, which will become apparent only as they are used.

In the technique of bobbin lacemaking, both directions of thread movement occur, but the cross (S) involves only one pair and so has only half the force of the twist (Z) involving two pairs[54]. Thus overall, throughout the thousands of cross and twist sequences which make up a bobbin lace, each twist will partially unwind an S-spun thread, while each cross will, as it were, restore its stability.

If on the other hand, a thread with a final Z-spin is used, this delicate balance may be lost. The lace may curl up on itself and refuse to lie flat, or the threads may unwind, or overtwist. Yet the entire beauty of a lace lies in its visible clarity of form, harmony of design, perfection of stitch and evenness of tension – all of which are inevitably threatened when uncooperative threads fight the lacemaker's attempts to manipulate them.

The lacemaker may fight back, by constantly turning the bobbins as she works so that tension is not allowed to build up in the thread; or she may wind the thread on the bobbin-necks in the reverse direction. Just such a problem must have faced bobbin lacemakers in the nineteenth century as they began to switch from hand-spun Z/plyed S linen to machine-spun cotton. England had led the way in the mechanical spinning of cotton, which was traditionally in a Z-direction for weaving. Cotton was England's most important article of trade, it was inexpensive, its use on bobbinet and warp-knitting machines was established by 1808, and it was only natural that bobbin lacemakers should experiment with it at a much earlier date than any continental European country where linen thread was, for the most part, more easily available. However, the actual date when cotton threads began to be manufactured specifically for handmade lace is unknown, and it is at least possible that the problems of the pioneers in this field resulted from the use of hard-twisted threads originally intended for warps.

The winding of thread onto English bobbins in a clockwise, in contrast to the continental anti-clockwise direction (fig. 53), may have originated at this time. The rings of spangles, such a unique feature of East Midlands (Bucks point) bobbins, may also have been aimed at stopping them from rolling uncontrollably about on the pillow, wracked by their thread contortions. The extra weight would also help to pull the threads straight, eliminating minor kinks.

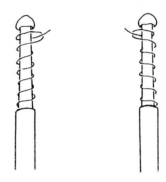

53. Clockwise and anti-clockwise bobbin winding. Left, continental; right, English. These traditional directions may at times be reversed to harmonize with differently spun threads.

Another alternative of course would be to work the crosses and twists in the reverse direction, i.e. crosses right to left, and twists left to right: an essay that was disastrous with an S-spun yarn should be entirely satisfactory with a Z. That this does indeed work is demonstrated by the traditional warp-twisting or four-part braiding of Danish Hedebo. The long warp ends left as a fringe when the woven linen is taken off the loom are picked up four at a time, in double pairs, beginning at the left hand side and working horizontally, instead of diagonally as in bobbin laces. Twists are S-orientated and crosses Z. The resultant fabric looks very like a bobbin lace although, in addition to the reversals of direction, it differs in having no pinholes and in the clothstitch threads lying slantwise instead of straight on (fig. 54a,b).

61

54.a. The thread movements of Hedebo warp-plaiting

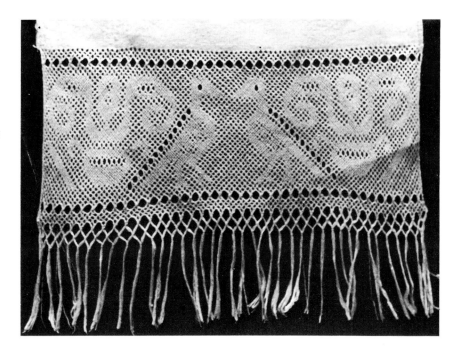

54.b. A completed border
(Nationalmuseet,
Copenhagen).

With regard to needle laces, the primitive looping worked spirally from a centre point, in a three-dimensional manner, allowed the direction of closure to be the same throughout the work (see fig. 43f), and the addition of short lengths one at a time prevented any unfavourable tensions from accumulating. In needle laces worked flat in a two-dimensional manner, the looping stitches must reverse their direction in alternate rows, so that whatever fibre they are made with, an adverse effect in one row will automatically be neutralized by a counteracting effect in the following.

In the *detached buttonhole stitch with a straight return*, also worked flat, there is a problem, since only alternate rows consist of looping. Thus the direction in which the loops are made is the same every time (fig. 55a-c).

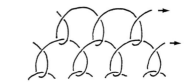

55. Detached buttonhole stitch:

a. Spiral looping. In the aborigine bag (see fig.43f) the S-spun yarns have a Z closure.

b. Flat looping: the loop closure is S and Z in alternate rows.

c. two-dimensional detached buttonhole stitch with a straight return. The loop closures are all the same.

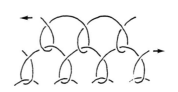

The lacemaker can proceed in four different ways, by working the loops;

1.  (a)   From R to L with the needle pointing away;
    (b)   From L to R with the needle pointing towards;
          Both give an **S** closure.
2.  (a)   From R to L with the needle pointing towards;
    (b)   From L to R with the needle pointing away;
          Both give a **Z** closure. (figs. 55d–g).

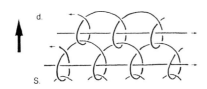

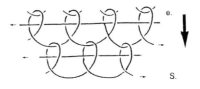

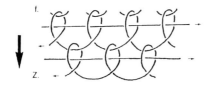

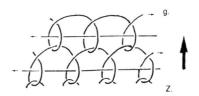

d. 1(a);   e. 1(b);   f. 2(a);   g. 2(b).

The vital question is: which method will work best with an S-spun thread, and which with a Z-spun? To investigate this with any thoroughness, three factors must be taken into consideration:

(a) The initial spin, and the direction of the ply if any.

(b) The balance of the ply, i.e. to what extent the distortion of the fibres by the single spin is eased or exacerbated by the second. Also how many times the thread is plyed.

(c) The twists or turns per inch or per millimetre. Turns always contract the thread up to 5% of its original length, and may either narrow or broaden it. In machine-spinning, the amount of twist inserted is determined by the speed of turning of the spindles in relation to the amount of yarn produced. For example, 10,208 revolutions per minute combined with a delivery of 465 inches of yarn per minute, gives a twist of 22 t.p.i.[55] But the t.p.i. can also be geared to the yarn number or count required for a particular end-use, the correct twist for 2-fold being the square root of the count multiplied by 3; or for 3-fold threads, by 2.3. For example[56]:

| Count | 10 | 2-fold | 9.5 t.p.i. | 3-fold | 7.3 t.p.i. |
|-------|----|--------|-----------|--------|-----------|
| | 30 | | | | 12.6 |
| | 50 | 22 | | | |
| | 100 | 30 | | | 23 |

Thus, broadly speaking, the thicker the thread, the fewer the twists, and vice versa. At the same time, the longer the fibres the fewer the turns needed to hold them together. Some threads may need to be hard spun (many twists) such as those for the 'brass bobbins' of lace machines. On the other hand, soft thick embroidery threads of gassed cotton from supercombed fibres might be 6-ply 2-fold initially spun S, plyed S with 10 t.p.i., then twisted 6-ply Z with one-and-a-half turns[57]. Up to a certain point, the closer the twist the stronger the yarn, since the fibres are made to press more tightly against each other, but above that limit the pull on the fibres becomes intolerable and the thread weakens.

These considerations mean that the success or otherwise of a thread for use with a particular lace is not easy to predict. The final direction of spin can be observed and the final turns per inch counted, but it is never visually obvious to what extent spin and ply are balanced, and therefore to what extent the further rotations introduced by lacemaking will disturb them.

Returning to an examination of needle laces, and the solid areas of design composed of detached buttonhole stitches with a straight return, either close or open form, a short cut to what might be a satisfactory thread for making them can be taken via an examination of good quality laces of the past, or of the detailed directions, and materials recommended, for making them, which were printed in *Needlecraft*, *Weldons* or *DMC* booklets, and which presumably were satisfactory:

1. In Thérèse de Dillmont's *Encyclopaedia of Needlework*, an S-twist linen thread is used for method 1(b): S-twist, S-closure.

2. In several examples of Youghal laces, S-spun or S-plyed cotton threads were worked by method 1(a): S-twist, S-closure.

3. The results of investigation of a range of laces, from the point of view of fibre, twist, loop-closure and turns per inch are summarized in table 5 and fig. 56. Where the stitches were not too closely packed, the straight return threads could be seen clearly enough to study the spin and ply and to get a rough estimate of the turns per unit length for comparison. It was also sometimes possible to locate unworked threads on the reverse side of the lace, and their crisp narrow appearance was in marked contrast to the worked (looped) threads which were found to be changed by the lacemaking process, being noticeably broader and less twisted, occasionally to such an extent that the fibres appeared to lie almost straight as if they had never been spun at all. Particularly in the combinations of S-twist and Z-closure, the looping movement had almost undone the ply, so that the worked threads looked like singles, though in the unworked threads from the same area, the ply was perfectly clear, and the turns quite easily counted.

4. In general, loop closure was in the Z direction, but a combination of final S-spin or twist with S-closure occurred in a number of cases without any apparent ill effect. In fact the Venetian and Youghal laces were of the highest quality, while the quantity of lace of this type produced negates any possibility of a freak success. In hand-spinning, which must apply to all lace threads prior to 1800, the spinner was not bound by fixed twist numbers, and could practise a flexibility impossible under machine automation; while the later laces, though constrained by machine-spun yarn, were basing their techniques as closely as possible upon Venetian models. It is possible too that the professional lacemakers may have turned their needles just sufficiently with each stitch to reinstate the original tension. This is speculation, but the superb quality of the laces themselves cannot be questioned.

64

**Table 5**      DETACHED BUTTONHOLE STITCH WITH A STRAIGHT RETURN

| DATE | LACE | FIBRE | SPIN/PLY | LOOP CLOSURE | TURNS/MM |
|------|------|-------|----------|--------------|----------|
| 4200BC (see fig.1) | Looping (needle-binding) | Willow bark (bast) | Z | S | |
| c1600 (fig.56) | Reticella | Linen | 2S plyed S<br>3S plyed S | S | 1.5 |
| 1650-1700 | Venetian gros point | Linen | Spin almost straight, S-plyed, like S singles | S | singles <14<br>2-ply = 8 |

The densely-worked solid design areas have a very firm almost hard texture, but because of the extensive openwork, bridged only by rare bars, the lace hangs well and looks graceful.

| DATE | LACE | FIBRE | SPIN/PLY | LOOP CLOSURE | TURNS/MM |
|------|------|-------|----------|--------------|----------|
| Late 17th C | Ven. coralline | Linen | 2S plyed S | S | 5 |
| c1700 | Point de France | Linen | S singles or weak ply | Z | 9-11 |
| Early 18th C | Point de Sedan | Linen | S singles | Z | 6-10 |
| c1760 | Argentan | Linen | S singles or 2S plyed S | Z | 9-14 |
| Second half 18th C | Alencon | Linen | 2S plyed S, some S singles | Z | 15-18 |
| First half 18th C | Reseau Venise | Linen | 2S plyed S | Z | 9-10 |
| c1900 | Burano copy of 17C Ven. gros pt. | Cotton (brown) | Weakly Z plyed S | Z | 6-8 |
| 19th-20th C | Point de gaze | Cotton | 2S plyed S, ply not clearly visible | Z | 10-12 |
| 20th C | Belgian point de Venise | Cotton (texture stiff and hard) | 2S plyed S | Z | 6-7 |
| c1900 | Youghal | Cotton | 2S plyed S or thick S singles | S (some Z) | 5-6 (more in thicker yarns) |
| c1900 | Ruskin cutwork | Cotton/linen | 2Z plyed S (woven area Z) | Z | could not be counted in looped areas |

Reticella c1600

point de France c1700

56. Needle laces from Table 5, showing S or Z closures in relation to yarn or thread turns. All are at the same magnification.

Venetian gros point, 17th century

Venetian coralline

point de Sedan

Argentan

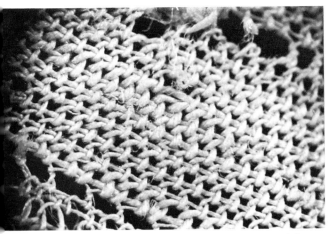
Alencon, 18th century. Note the very fine threads, bottom left.

point de gaze.

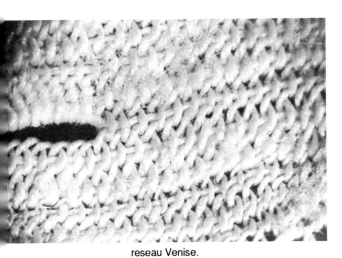
reseau Venise.
Burano lace, late 19th century.

Belgian point de Venise, 20th century.
Youghal.

Of the machine threads, a large number suitable for weaving or other sinks, are not suitable for laces. Fuzziness or knobbliness which may be an aesthetic advantage in woven or knitted textiles is a total disadvantage as far as lace is concerned. In face each end-use requires its own special thread. For hand-sewing the threads are S-spun singles, or Z plyed S, since the rotatory nature of the stitch movements, as in needle laces, add or subtract twists of their own, and a final Z twist would kink during use[58]. Threads for machine-sewing are S plyed Z; cotton for lace-making (brass bobbin yarns) are Z plyed S; while crochet cotton is doubled twice, ZSZ. All sewing threads were in fact of silk until 1806 when Napoleon I threatened to go to war with any country that traded with England. In response, Clarks of Paisley developed a sewing yarn of cotton which, by 1826, was in popular use[59]. Silk filament threads, adapted for the sewing machine in 1852, were marketed as 'machine twist' to distinguish them from 'sewing silks' intended for hand use. 'Floss silks', intended for embroidery, were made of waste silk staples spun softly, with few twists, since the more perfect the 'state of parallelism' of the fibres in the finished thread the higher would be the lustre.

For laces, threads need to be:

(a) Strong enough to survive the strenuous friction and manipulation they must undergo as the lace is constructed.

(b) Of small diameter to produce the 'slender' fabric.

(c) Flexible enough to be moved, bent, twisted, knotted and curled as required by the lace stitches, yet resistant to deformation. Some threads (silk) may glide too easily over each other so that the stitches made by them slip out of place and upset the tension. Metals are too stiff, intractable and rough-surfaced for closely interlocked work. Wool, because of its scales which catch against each other, is rarely used except for rather coarse and simple bobbin laces. Cotton is satisfactory for most laces, though the tips of its short fibres tend to spill out from their tight twist with the friction of the multitudinous cross-twist repetitions, or of loopings, not to mention the traumatic events of wash and wear that must follow. Synthetics are recent, and have no part in antique laces. A certain cold rigidity, which can change into over-plasticity with high temperatures, makes them at this time less popular than they will doubtless become.

Linen alone – strong, smooth, long-fibred, moisture-absorbing, lustrous and with excellent drape – is ideal for all types of lace. It is little harmed by friction (abrasion resistance), by hand it can be spun loosely to give a soft yet firm texture, or more tightly when a crisp clarity is required. It was linen alone, with its antipathy to stable dyes, which, throughout its long period of popularity, created the myth that lace must be white. The reverence of the ancient Egyptians for the beauty of linen was so profound that they deified the flax plant as a creation of the goddess Isis. This tradition of some supernatural mystique continued through the use of linen for religious ceremonies in Israel, Greece, Rome and the Roman Catholic church, an attitude paralleled by the adoration of the Peruvian Indians for their own celestially personified plant fibre, cotton[60].

These exclusive and incomparable fibres inevitably bestow on the laces made from them all their sight- and touch-qualities of drape, colour, lustre, lightness, coolness or warmth, flexibility or rigidity; and all their properties of durability, water-absorption and abrasion-resistance; along with their vulnerability or otherwise to light, insects, acids and alkalis. The thread chosen affects not only the appearance of the lace, but its survival during use. It determines how it should be handled, worn, cleaned and stored.

### Less common fibres and their use in lacemaking

PINEAPPLE (*Ananas comosus*) (fig. 57a). The glossily sheer pina (pronounced penya) cloth, woven from pineapple fibres, was highly valued both in itself and as the perfect base for the setting of priceless hand embroideries[61]. In the Philippines, crisp lustrous scarves and cloths embroidered in pulled thread-work with exotic designs of luscious fruits and flowers, were made from it, using an amazing variety of stitches (fig. 57b,c).

57.a. Pineapple leaves, from which the fibres are taken.

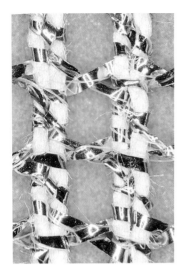

4. Lurex 'gold' foil around a synthetic fibre core. A bobbinet by John Heathcoat (photo: Rowena Gale).

7. Henrietta Maria, after Van Dyck, c1625. Note the grey tint of the collar and cuffs (courtesy: National Portrait Gallery, London).

18d. A bobbin lace made of silk, reputedly from spiders.

36. Fine woollen singles used to knit a Shetland shawl.

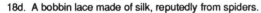

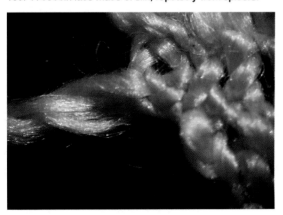

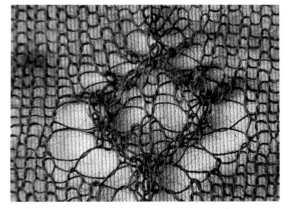

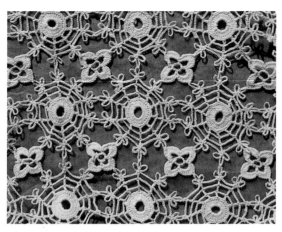

38. Strips of silver foil wound around a cotton core.

41f. Chainstitch, crochet.

41b. Bebilla, flowers in coloured silk.

43a. Cutwork.

43f. An Australian tucker bag made of bush string, stitches as 43c. The bark of sapling trees is chewed, pounded and twined before being looped (Mimi Aboriginal Arts and Crafts, Northern Territories, 1980s).

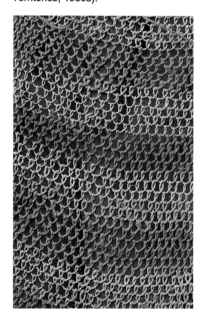

49a. Genoese c1600: there is no clear distinction between solid design and openwork ground areas.

58b. A Brazilian bobbin weighted with an immature coconut.

51. Russian bobbin lace of coloured silks and precious metal, 19th century.

65. A 16th century drawnwork. Around the plain weave areas of the design, selected warps and wefts have been cut away, the raw edges oversewn and the remaining strands bound around with crimson silk (courtesy: Ora Humberd).

75. Bobbin lace made from pig bristles, Queyras (courtesy: Lysiane Brulet).

66c. The lace of the collar and bodice neck may have been worked with bobbins to a Parasole design, but a delicate needle lace is more likely (see fig.66a). The matching cuffs are backed by red silk.
(Courtesy: The Frick Art Museum).

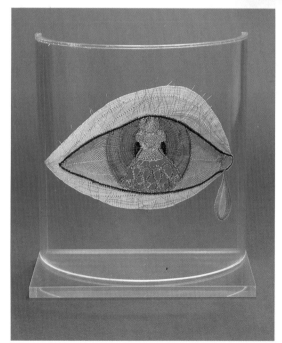

80. *The Eye of Midas,* by Dewi Wong (Pittsburgh), 1988. The king's young daughter, mirrored in his eye, is turned by his glance into a statue of gold. Filled with remorse, he weeps. (Bobbin lace techniques in three-dimensional mode, mounted in perspex or plexiglas. Worked with 'Japan gold' of nylon and polyester, Z-plyed Indian art silk, and multicoloured metallic thread composed of nylon, metal foil and pure silver).

76. A tourist souvenir: a selection of native plants stuck to a circle of lace bark. Jamaica, 20th century.

57.b. A scarf or table runner of pina cloth, showing an opulent design in pulled threadwork.

c. Detail.

BANANA   According to the Women's Institute book, *Sewing Materials*, *c*1930, 'Fiber lace is made from the fibres of the banana and aloe plant. It is a frail expensive lace and is not practical for many purposes – but both are used for dress trimmings especially on sheer organdies and chiffons'. In Brazil, banana leaf fibres were used for bobbin laces similar to the 'palm' borders still made in Portugal (fig. 57d). The fibres were joined end to end with a weaver's knot.

PITA fibre, or *Aloe*, is obtained from the leaf of the century plant, *Agave americana*, a member of the same family as Pineapple, growing in Central and South America and in Mexico. The fibres are 3 to 7 feet long, light in weight and slightly crinkly. They are used in the Azores to make a delicate knitted lace. Aloe was used for crochet and for bobbin laces in the 1850s and 60s (figs. 58a,b in colour).

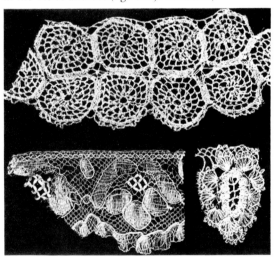

58. a. Above and right, crochet (? aloe fibre); below left, a bobbin lace (coconut leaves).

COIR (*Cocos nucifera*).   Apart from cotton, the only other seed fibre with even the remotest connection with lace is the fibrous material which pads the coconut fruit, enabling it to float on water. The coarse reddish-brown strands of coir measure 10 inches in length and some 16 to 19 microns in diameter, being made up of minute ultimates 0.4 to

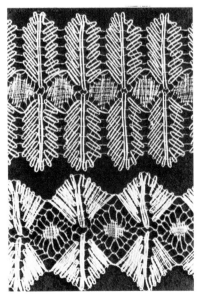

57.d.  Lace borders with fan and palm motifs, possibly made of banana leaf fibres.

1mm long. They are stiff and wiry, and rather unlikely candidates for lacemaking, though there is a connection in that Brazilian bobbins may be weighted with the tiny coconuts which fall undeveloped from the trees (fig. 58c,d), and the leaf fibres may have limited local use.

58a(i). detail of crochet

(ii) detail of bobbin lace

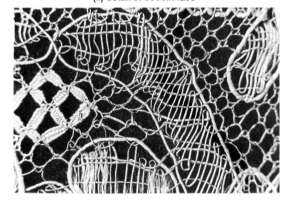

PALM    The cuticle or outermost layer of the young leaves of the Raphia palm (*Raphia ruffia*), found in Madagascar, can be peeled off to provide flat fibre-like strips 3 to 4 feet long and half-an-inch wide, and these can be split lengthwise into finer filaments, about 14 microns across (see fig. 25d).

A similar fibre, known as *pita de corojo* is obtained from the Macaw palm of Brazil. Internal fibres from the unopened leaves of the Tucun palm are used for very fine knitting.

Yet other Palm fibres bear a close resemblance to horsehair, for example *crin végétal* (vegetable horse-hair) from an Algerian dwarf palm. The same name is applied to fibres from a parasitic plant of the tropics known as Spanish Moss, which is related to the pineapple[62].

STRAW, the crushed and dried stems of grass, reeds or cereals was used in Switzerland in combination with horsehair, or even with silk, imparting glints of pale gold (fig. 58e,f).

In fact, all kinds of obscure varieties of tropical plants were used to make tourist laces. Even if their names were known, unfamiliarity would render them meaningless. But the novel effects which they produce suggest ideas for experimentation.

(Fig.58b see colour pages)

c. Straw on net, probably French.

d. Twisted straw used to make a braid, Swiss.

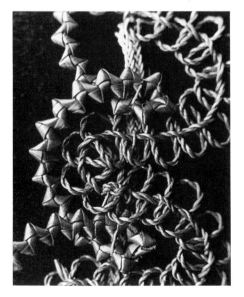

70

The tendency of lace to wallow in a mire of complicated and ambiguous terminology is evident even in what might be thought the straightforward nomenclature of thread-supplying plants. *Pita* has been applied to several, other than the century plant, for example Sisal (*Agave sisalana*), silk grass (*Bromelia magdalanae*), *Ananas macrodontes* which provides thick fibres for cordage, and Mauritius hemp. It overlaps the name Aloe, used not only of the fibres of *Agave americana*, but also of those of Mauritius hemp (*Fourcroya foetida*). There are at least six quite different plants sharing the name hemp: Sunn or Indian Hemp (*Crotalaria juncea*); Hemp (*Cannabis*); Swedish Hemp (*Urtica*); Guinea Hemp or Kenaf (*Hibiscus cannabinus*); Manila Hemp or Abaca (*Musa textilis*); and New Zealand Hemp (*Phormium tenax*). The first four are bast, the last two leaf, fibres. In the past, hemp was often referred to as 'linen'.

**HORSEHAIR** One of the earliest records of the use of horsehair is a braided or plaited belt from county Antrim in Ireland, dated by pollen analysis to the late Bronze Age (900–600 BC). Though the belt is not itself openwork, braiding was the technique adopted by lace in sixteenth-century passements, and later in Genoese and other bobbin laces. Horsehair was used for peasant headdresses in Switzerland (fig. 59a). Though flexible, it is stiff to work and does not wind easily on to bobbins, so that designs are simple, and usually geometric. The hair from the mane of the Prince Imperial (see fig. 24), was eight-and-a-half foot long, but this is a record: half that length is more usual. Joins must therefore be frequent and the springy fibres are tied with difficulty by overhand knots. Being thick (113 to 233 microns in diameter), single hairs were used to support the picots, and sometimes also the ground, of Alençon needle laces, so that the loops would be equal in size, and the rows of stitches straight (fig. 59b).

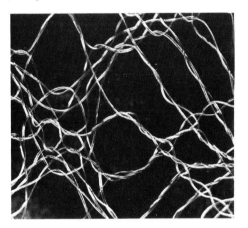

59a. Bobbin lace made from horsehair. Note that the hair is not spun, but used as a monofilament.
b. Horsehair used to support the picots of Alencon needle lace, c1860s. The single hair is thicker than the cotton thread of the design area.

Viscose rayon factories in Nottingham, and at Emmenbrucke in Switzerland, marketed a product called crinol which could be used in place of real horsehair. Though chemically a regenerated cellulose instead of a protein as in the equine form, it looks very similar and has the advantage that it can be made to whatever length the manufacturer requires. There remains the restriction that the necks of bobbins can hold only a limited length of thread, and joining knots would still appear in the handmade lace. A considerable yardage of 'horsehair' lace without joins indicates not only synthetic yarn but also machine manufacture, most probably on Barmen machines where the fully-wound spindles hold very considerable quantities. Additional springiness can be achieved by making the fibres in a bicomponent form, that is two fibres are spun side by side through adjacent spinnerets and welded together as they emerge (fig. 60).

**HUMAN HAIR** When horsehair as a temporary support is too coarse, human hair may replace it, as in the picots of the ultra-fine seventeenth-century Venetian laces. It was also sometimes used, probably for or by sailors, to make intensely personal momentos of a sentimental nature (fig. 61).

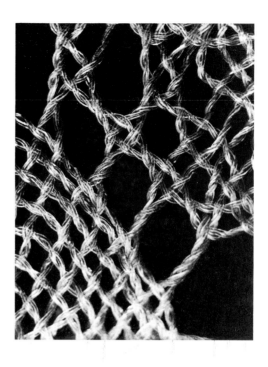

60. 'Bicomponent' synthetic thread in a Barmen machine lace.

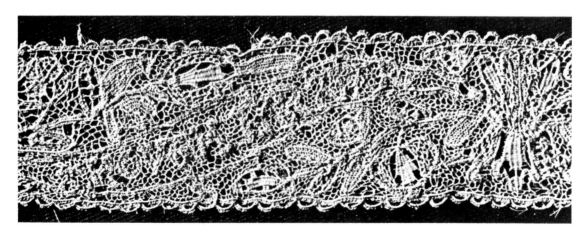

61. *Though far apart (yet neere in heart).* A needle lace souvenir made of human hair.

# 9 *How thick is a thread?*

From the point of view of lace, the thread's diameter is very important, since it determines the space it will take up. This in turn affects the size of the stitches, and stitches must be a particular size or they will not fit the pattern. With too thick a thread the lace will look cramped and congested, with too thin a thread it will be flabby and slack.

A lace cannot look right if the thread is wrong.

For ease of reference, the thickness of many lace threads is indicated by a number, often referred to as the *yarn number* or *count*, its assessment being a counting process during which the yarn is reeled from the spindle on to a rotating wheel turned 560 times to produce a *hank* or *lea*.

Unfortunately for lucidity, the circumference of the wheel used is not always the same. In worsted, for example, it is 36 inches (one yard) in circumference, so that each hank is 560 yards long, while for cotton it is 54 inches (one-and-a-half yards) in circumference, so that 560 turns will give a hank 840 yards long[63].

For any type of spun yarn, the number of hanks, each produced by 560 turns of the wheel, which make up a one pound weight, constitutes the count of that yarn. In other words count, as applied to yarns made of spun (staple) fibres, expresses variation in length in relation to a fixed weight. Such yarns include not only wool, cotton and linen, but mercerized cotton, spun silk, spun rayon and spun synthetics.

The horrifying chaos prevalent throughout the counting systems of all the main yarns at the end of the nineteenth century is conveyed by an article, 'The Counts of Yarns', in the *Textile Educator* of 1889. At that time, at least eleven different systems were in operation for wool alone. Linen counts – the number of hanks, each 300 yards long needed to make up one pound weight – were the only ones 'which had been interfered with or governed by law in this country'. Over a range of yarns, all labelled as 20s count, the number of yards actually contained in one pound could vary between 320,000 (raw silk) and 320 (Dewsbury wool), and the author realized

that 'this points very clearly to the desirability of having some fixed and recognized standard of measurement for the counts of yarns . . . It would seem as though the decimal system would be the simplest, and the one upon which calculations might be most easily worked'.

One hundred years later, such a system *is* established, in Tex. Logical, but unpopular, it is still far from being universally exploited and, as lacemakers will know, the systems for numbering cotton and other threads remain depressingly diverse.

The metric system has long been operational for yarns made from filament fibres (silk, man-made fibres and synthetics), where a variable weight in grams is related to a fixed length in metres. The unit here is not a count, but a *denier*. In 1900, the so-called 'Italian system' was adopted internationally, using 450 metres as the standard length to be weighed[64]. This has since been changed to 9,000 metres. If 9,000 metres of nylon for example weigh 15 grams, that yarn will be described as 15-denier.

The two systems obviously work in different ways. Counts are *indirect* in the sense that the thicker the yarn, the fewer hanks will be needed to weigh one pound, and therefore the lower the count will be. The denier system is *direct*. The thicker the yarn, the more grams 9,000 metres of it will weigh, and the higher its denier will be.

The problem with regard to international standardization has always been the enormously extensive and expensive replacement of precision-made weighing and measuring equipment, often incorporated into the spinning machines, which would be needed to make the change from one system to another.

Tex, first introduced in the 1940s, and officially adopted in 1964, is, like denier, a direct system. It applies to all yarns and expresses the weight in grams of 1,000 metres. In spite of its rationality, conversions between Tex and long-established units can involve quite complicated arithmetic.

Equivalents between the varying staple counts on the other hand are no great problem. For example:

In a 100-count cotton yarn, (100 × 840) yards weigh one pound. To find the equivalent count in linen yarn, divide: (100 × 840) by 300. The linen count is 280. To find the equivalent in worsted yarn, divide the (100 × 840) by 560. The worsted count is 150.

Tables of equivalents exist for relating counts to both Tex and denier. Thus the British Standards publication no. 4985 (1973):

| English cotton | Denier (silk, rayon) | Tex | Metric | Worsted | Linen |
|---|---|---|---|---|---|
| 40 | 132 | 14 | 70 | 60 | 118 |
| 60 | 88 | 9.5 | | | |
| 100 | 53 | 6 | | | |
| 120 | 44 | 5 | 200 | | |
| 180 | 29 | 3 | | | |
| 350 | 15 | 1.5 | | | |

### Calculating yarn counts

The counts and deniers of yarns can be set automatically during machine spinning. A problem for lace-makers however may be to equate modern yarns with those found in antique laces, should they wish to copy them. Lacemaking may either tighten or slacken the twist of a thread, making it thinner or thicker than it was before the work began, so that measurements of thread *in* a lace do not necessarily indicate the yarn number that was originally chosen. Additionally, threads marketed under the same yarn number can vary in their turns per inch, and this affects the hardness or softness of the finished lace. Though loose and compacted threads may weigh the same per unit length, the compacted or hard spun are thinner and will work up as if their number were higher.

Also, threads are not flat two-dimensional structures, but three-dimensional cylinders: they have volume, not area. In other words they have *density*, that is mass per unit volume, measured in grams and cubic centimetres, at standard temperature and pressure. Or, to put it simply, some yarns are denser or more solid than others, and their hanks will weigh more, even though their thickness of thread is the same.

In practise, the figure quoted is not density but *specific gravity*, or the density of the fibre in relation to that of water, taken as 1. Conveniently, all the cellulose fibres are much the same, the specific gravity of linen, cotton and rayon being 1.5. For the protein fibres silk and wool, and also for cellulose acetate, it is 1.3; for nylon, 1.1[65]. In the interests of accuracy, it should be added that these figures relate

to the pure chemicals, and may be slightly out for the fibres themselves which always contain some impurities in the form of gums, lignin etc.

A method of calculating the count of antique linen yarns was demonstrated by von Henneberg in 1931[66]. He measured the diameter of a yarn known to have a count of 210, and found it to be 105 microns. The micron (often written $\mu$, pronounced *mew*) is equivalent to one-thousandth of a millimetre, and is the traditional unit of microscopic measurement.

He then measured the diameter of an antique (*c*1700) yarn, and found it to be 45 microns. He calculated as follows: The count of the yarn represents the number of hanks which will weigh one pound. In other words,

volume of one hank × count = 1 pound.

The volume of the hank is represented by the formula:

area of circular cross-section × length of 1 hank

*or* $\tau r^2 \times$ length

where r = half the measured diameter, and length (for linen) = 300 yards.

Then:

Modern yarn:
$$(\tau \times 52.5^2 \times 300) \times 210 = 1 \text{ pound.}$$
Antique yarn:
$$(\tau \times 22.5^2 \times 300) \times N = 1 \text{ pound.}$$

where N = the unknown count of the antique yarn. Since $\tau$ and 300 occur on both sides, they can be eliminated. Then,

$$22.5^2 \times N = 52.5^2 \times 210$$

and

$$N = \frac{52.5^2 \times 210}{22.5^2} = 1,200.$$

Taking the linen fibre as having a minimum diameter of 12 microns (Matthews), this means that a 1,200 count yarn would contain only 14 fibres:

$$\frac{(\text{radius of yarn})^2}{(\text{radius of fibre})^2} = \frac{22.5^2}{6^2} = 14.$$

Contrariwise, the fibre diameter can be calculated from diameters of threads, and fibre numbers, in various laces (see Table 6), though truly accurate counting is quite difficult. For example, seventeenth-century Venetian gros point threads, with diameters of 50 to 70 microns, were found to contain 16 to 28 fibres. Then:

$$\text{area of fibre section} = \frac{\text{area of thread section}}{\text{numbers of fibres}}$$

so:

$$(\tau)\ r^2\ \text{fibre} = \frac{(\tau)\ r^2\ \text{thread}}{16} = \frac{25^2}{16} = 39$$

radius = 6.25        diameter of fibre = 12.5 microns.

Such calculations, although they cannot take into account the full effect of the manufacturing (weaving or lace-making) processes, can still be immeasurably helpful not only in lace but for example in estimating comparative counts of archeological finds. Warps threads per centimetre width, counted in Egyptian woven linens of 3000 to 2000 BC, were found to number 130. Assuming them to be closely packed, the diameter of each thread would be 77 microns, equivalent to a count of 390.

It is clear that comparisons *can* be made simply by measuring yarns or thread widths with the greatest possible accuracy. Although 'simply' is perhaps not quite the right word.

The measurement has to be taken with a graticule, or eyepiece micrometer, and adjusted in accordance with the magnification used. Since the thread is three-dimensional it cannot, under the microscope, all be in focus at the same time, so that its side limits may be difficult to distinguish with exactitude. At the same time, the refractive index between the thread and the air around it will distort the light rays and perhaps lead to false readings. If the thread is mounted in a liquid such as glycerine to eliminate this hazard, it introduces further ones, namely that the fibre may absorb moisture and swell, so appearing thicker than it really is; or the pressure of the cover slip (which should then be placed over the thread to prevent the liquid coming into contact with the microscope objective) will inevitably squash it slightly, again artificially enlarging its width. The thickness as seen under the microscope is not necessarily the same as the diameter: fibres may be bean-shaped or oval in cross-section, and although the process of spinning does normally produce a cylindrical thread, the constancy of its thickness will be interrupted by twists. The smoother the thread, the less important this latter problem will be. It does however make it necessary for several measurements – 50 to 100 are recommended – to be taken from different parts of the yarn to allow for possible variations. These will then be eliminated by averaging the results (fig. 62a). Such hair-splitting considerations apart, where it is not possible to get the count of the yarn directly – because it has been used and is now part of a lace – diameter measurements taken with reasonable accuracy may give an adequate working guide.

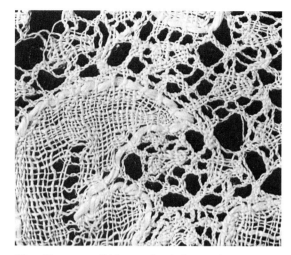

62. a. The uneven thickness of early linen and cotton yarns: (i) Binche bobbin lace c1700; (ii) Peruvian loom lace with added weft patterning, c1100 AD (courtesy: Museum for Textiles, Toronto).

Where more precision is required, a projection microscope and screen of squared paper used at a known magnification (say ×500) enable the width to be measured by counting the squares. Alternatively a micronaire technique, using a special instrument, provides a measurement by forcing air through a loosely packed mass of the fibres[67]. Micronaire readings are used in the cotton industry to relate diminishing fineness to maturity, and fibre dimensions to Tex[68].

For the practising lacemaker, measurements of approximate count by diameters is valid, but only for comparative purposes where absolute accuracy is neither possible nor aimed for: 'Single threads are approximately cylinders. But as the sections in any one thread are not uniform, and are difficult to measure, it is found totally impracticable to number yarns in the same way as wires are gauged, i.e. proportional, directly or indirectly, to their diameters'[69].

It could be postulated, following the arithmetic set out on p. 74, that a linen count of 1,200 would be equivalent to a British Standards cotton count of:

$$\frac{1200 \times 300}{840} = \text{approximately } 430.$$

An article in *The Lace and Embroidery Review* of Jan.–June 1911 describes a cotton yarn of count 420 being produced by the English firm of Thomas Oliver in Macclesfield. A pound weight of such a yarn would cover more than 200 miles. This yarn, fine as the buoyant wisps of flax two hundred years before, was spun not by hand but by machine – which scarcely lessened the difficulties of its manufacture. Firstly, the longest possible fibres had to be used, to draw out to sufficient fineness, and at the same time to have adequate tensile strength to make a usable thread. According to the article, four-inch or longer staples from the delicate Sea Island cotton grown on the sandy islands off Georgia and South Carolina, or in the West Indian island of Anguila, were used. The spinning rooms of the factory were hung around with blankets kept constantly dripping wet – reminiscent of the cellars and cowsheds provided for the human spinners of flax in more ancient times. The need for a certain temperature – to control the absorption of water by the fibres and to prevent any expansion of the metal parts of the machines where the minutest displacement might overstrain the yarn – was more difficult to achieve in the days before the First World War when electricity was still quite young: the first Electric Lighting Act was passed in 1882, and thermostats although developed in a primitive form in the 1830s were not available for large-scale air-conditioning until very much later. So important was this temperature/humidity factor that the yarn could not be spun to order and the factory could only add to its stock as conditions permitted.

After gassing, the yarn was flattened so that more could be held on the bobbins of the Leavers lace machines to produce the entrancing 'bobbin finings' (fig. 62b) so popular in the twenties, until supplies ran out and the Sea Island cotton plants themselves were annihilated by the boll weevil, and their products joined the long line of laces which, through lack of suitable thread, will never be made again.

Wakefield, describes the spinning of cotton for the 'brass bobbin threads' of the lace machines as the *bête noire* of the trade[70]:

'Above 100/2, the fineness of the single yarn necessitates great care in the spinning and the selection of the fibres . . . the still higher numbers, 220/2 to 400/2 form a reserved class, into the company whereof one enters with bated breath. Few doublers have attempted a 250/2 gassed, and fewer still have seen a 300/2 or 400/2 thread . . . The super fine singles for 400s is entirely beyond the reach of ordinary mortals . . . in the superfine grades, high speeds are an impossibility'.

Both spinning and doubling had to be done slowly (by machine standards), producing a dramatic rise in labour costs. The Flyer, or Throstle, at a maximum speed of 4,000 revolutions per minute was used for the fine threads, while the coarser were doubled on the Ring Frame, at a speed of 5,000 r.p.m.

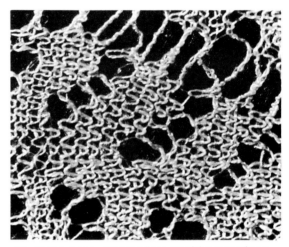

62b. Bobbin fining. Note the fineness of the cotton 'brass bobbin threads' which make the zigzag stitches.

The *Lace and Embroidery Review* article of 1911 continues, 'while these threads may not be said to be worth their weight in gold, they are at least worth their weight in silver. A pound of 420s is worth £6, that is 30 dollars'. At that time, American cotton-spinning machines could produce nothing finer than a 150s count, while their lace machines could use nothing finer than 260s. The sink for these exquisite Sea Island threads was machine laces, while coarser 120s threads were exported to France for hand lacemaking (fig. 62c).

Earlier, at the Philadelphia Exhibition of 1876, a 400s cotton thread, produced by the Willimantic Company of the USA from 'top quality Sea Island cotton', was described as 'the finest ever made'.

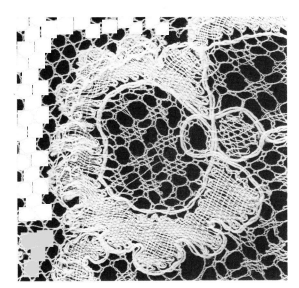

62c. A bobbin lace design appliqued to a machine net which has been cut away on the reverse side. Mid-19th century. The fine machine-spun cotton thread is used double in the solid design areas. (photo John Knight, courtesy: W.S.C.A.D.).

For silk laces, the spun or waste form was recommended in preference to the more expensive and less easy to handle filament yarn, with its slippery gloss. Some manufacturers classify silk yarns by letter instead of by number, e.g. A to D (Coats).

Worsted is not much used for laces. For any lacemaker wishing to try it, the numbering systems of different manufacturers are not easy to equate, and advice from a lace thread supplier would be of more practical value than any further information here.

The progressive decrease in fineness during the twentieth century is indicated in *Viscose Silk, c*1930s. It quotes 354s as the finest cotton count available at that time (equivalent to 15 denier); 400 as the finest English worsted (= 266 cotton); and the finest linen as 115 (approximately equivalent to 40s cotton, 60s wool and 130 denier). Von Henneberg in 1931 says that at the time of writing the highest linen count made by machine was 240, and by hand only 60 to 70, although only a few years previously counts of 300 to 400 had been available.

### The counts of plyed threads

When two or more yarns are twisted together, the resultant thread is thicker, and therefore of a lower count or higher denier. The process is called *folding*, *plying*, *twisting* or *doubling* – this latter regardless of the number of yarns or plys involved. The advantage

of plying is that is can produce a thread of greater strength, evenness, elasticity and stability than is possible with singles where a soft spin, by reducing the points of contact between the fibres, enables them to slip apart, severing the yarn, while on the other hand a hard spin may result in a dull harsh yarn which snarls and overtwists during working.

In plyed yarns there can be variations in:

(a)  the number plyed together;
(b)  the direction of spin of the original yarns, and of the twists of the ply;
(c)  the number of turns per inch in both yarn and thread;
(d)  the way that the ply is expressed.

With regard to this last feature, older authorities state quite categorically that 'when speaking of two-fold worsted or cotton, the actual count of the yarn is only half of what it is termed, thus in speaking of two-fold 60s [expressed 2/60s] the actual count of the thread is 30s'.

This is clear enough. However the expression of ply is not consistent. Wakefield, writing in 1916 says[71]: 'The count of the single yarn is written first, and separated by a stroke from the number of ends forming the folded thread, i.e. 60/2 − 30s'. Carter, also, quotes cotton threads of 40/2, 40/3 and 40/4 as of increasing coarseness, presumably with final counts of 20, 13 and 10.

In spun silk, 60/2 means two 120s plyed together, so that 60 represents not the original but the final thickness[72]. In filament silk and artificial silk, it is not unusual for the denier to be qualified, e.g. 150/70 means 150 denier made up of 70 filaments or strands.

Care has to be taken in plying a yarn that the resultant thread is properly *balanced*, that is the internal and external tensions set up in the thread by the additional spiralling must harmonize, not conflict, with each other. In fact the situation is quite complex, involving both direction of twist and turns per inch in the singles as well as in the plyed thread. It is helpful if the direction is incorporated in the expression of ply, for example:

$$2S/Z60s \quad \text{or} \quad Z60/2S$$

would mean two Z-spun singles of 60s count S-twisted to give a 2-ply 30s thread.

In hand-spinning, whether fine or coarse, the balance must be sensed by the spinner, and this has the advantage of immense flexibility of production. In machine-spinning, the most complicated calculations can be invoked, and the machine pre-set to produce not only balanced threads, but ones specifically adapted to a variety of sinks or end-uses, each taking into account the stresses which those threads must subsequently undergo during the processes of weaving, hand-sewing, machine-sewing, or hand- or machine-lacemaking.

To take an example of balancing threads[73]:

(a) If two singles with 24 S-turns per inch are plyed using 12 Z-turns per inch, the t.p.i. of the singles will be reduced to 12 (the 12 Z-turns having unspun 12 of the S-turns). Both singles and plyed thread now have a t.p.i. of 12, and the thread is balanced.

(b) If plying is increased to 24 Z-turns per inch, it will remove all the turns of the S-spun singles, making their fibres straight.

(c) If the Z-twisting continues to more than 24 t.p.i., not only will all the original S-spin of the singles be lost, but they will begin to turn in a Z direction, eliminating the evidence of the plying process. In effect, the final thread will look like a rather thick Z-spun single.

Each of these possibilities produces a different type of thread, and unfortunately the two features of lustre and strength, so desirable in an attractive lace, are sometimes mutually exclusive. Thus thread (a) will be soft, pliant, lustrous and silky, but will lack strength, elasticity and that compactness essential if a lace design is to stand out crisply from its surrounding ground. In thread (b), the original spins are further incorporated into the ply, but the tighter final twist reduces the lustre as it increases the strength. Thread (c) will be the strongest, but also the hardest and dullest; at the same time, the unspinning of the singles resulting from the reverse

twist of the ply will give fullness of texture since all the fibres are now running in the same direction.

The reversal of direction between spin and twist described above is much the commoner arrangement, but twist and ply in the same directions (S plyed S or Z plyed Z) does occur. This is far more likely to increase the tensions in the fibres instead of alleviating them, and the thread may well become *unbalanced*. It will kink and coil on itself, writhing as if to escape unbearable stress, until it is a misery for the lacemaker to use. For example, if 2 singles with 20 S-twists per inch are plyed using 10 S-twists per inch, the strain of the extra 10 is added to the original 20, and may become excessive.

But lace never ceases to mystify, and to make nonsense of our expectations. S-twist threads have been used to make needle laces with S loop-closures – surely a certain formula for disaster – and the product has been some of the loveliest laces ever created. See Table 5.

### Slender?

The thickness of threads is obviously very relevant to lace, not only because different counts suit different patterns but because lace is defined, in English, as 'a slender fabric'. At what point between fine and coarse 'slender' ceases to apply is difficult to determine. There is no sharp numerical cut-off point: the judgement is a subjective one. In art and craft, not everything can be delimited with precision, and there is nothing wrong with saying 'in my opinion', as long as that opinion can be backed up by sensible argument.

63. The first cotton handmade lace to be used in fashion: pulled threadwork, known as Dresden , 18th century.

# 10 *The whys and wherefores of fashion*

All the foundations of fibre selection and lace technique lie in prehistory. Thousands of years later there began a far shorter but momentously eventful recorded sequence of style and industrial development, in a milieu of competitively commercial marketing, and the compulsive need for change which this engendered to avoid saturation and stagnation. Shapes and positionings of lace accessories, as well as the types of fibre in vogue at any particular period – which in turn affected both design and texture – led to a kaleidoscope of apparently random variations in which one quality constantly replaced another as leading ingredient of the uniquely acceptable essence for that particular season.

The qualities of a lace are basically chemical (cellulose, protein or synthetic). Superimposed on these are the physical qualities of the fibres (shape and size in cross-section, surface and internal features, length etc). Further qualities are introduced as the fibres are turned into threads. Direction of twist, twists per inch, ply and count, all affect the ease with which the thread can be worked, as well as the texture and appearance of the finished lace. The conversion of the threads into lace adds qualities of tension, technique and design melded together by the lacemaker's skill.

Fickleness is an adjective almost inseparable from the concept of fashion. As shapes, sizes and proportions of clothes varied, so did the accessories, including lace. At specific times, a fair constancy of fashion existed across the countries of Europe – the active core from which all the types and fashions of lace emanated. These 'specific' times, appear as a series of steps down or up through the decades, each marked by changes, sometimes quite drastic, in styles of clothing and concepts of design, as well as in the threads and techniques used. Although the choice of thread depends to some extent on the locality of the production, the dominance of particular threads in lace fashion follow, broadly, a chronological sequence, each new fad rising to dominance as its predecessor was elbowed aside. In this chapter the fibres will be considered, not in their overall importance to lace, as heretofore, but in their historical succession of ascendency:

**Gold, silver**.  Sixteenth century. After that, the use of precious metal laces was restricted to formal occasions, the church, and certain geographical areas.

**Coloured silks**.  Sixteenth century. Bobbin passements and embroidered burattos. Mainly from north Italy. Silk accepts dyes more readily than any other fibre.

**Linen (hand-spun)**.  1550s to 1850: 300 years of white laces, since linen thread did not take dyes satisfactorily, its great capacity for water making the colours run. Black silks continued to be made in smallish quantities throughout this period, but brighter colours lost favour. Natural-coloured (blonde) silks were important in fashion from the 1760s to the 1860s, but linen remained pre-eminent. There were some eighteenth-century embroidered laces made in cotton (fig. 63).

**Cotton (machine-spun)**.  *c*1805 to the present day for machine nets and patterned laces. Little was used for handmade bobbin laces before 1830; or for needle laces before 1850. Its over-whiteness led to its being tinted an 'unbleached' (écru) colour, which led ultimately to a fashion for coloured laces, made by machine. However for handmade laces the attempts to pretend that cotton was undyeable linen continued for many decades, and the introduction, or reintroduction, of strong or even pastel shades other than tints of cream was strongly resisted.

**Synthetics**.  *c*1940s to the present day. They were increasingly used for machine laces not only because of the greater speed of production and lower cost of the yarn, but also because they were strong, elastic and easy to care for, though the earlier laces of this type tended to drape poorly and to feel clammy and harsh. The use of synthetics for handmade, non-fashion, laces produces an original effect sometimes markedly at variance with traditional forms.

The reason for the fairly clear-cut sequence summarized above is related to the availability of materials, the cost of the thread, historical events such as wars which imposed import and export restrictions on the countries involved, balance of trade deficits, economic depressions, national debts and other influences not directly connected with the laces themselves.

### *Precious metals*

The early popularity of gold for openwork braids and passements was linked with the huge influx of precious metals from the Spanish conquests in the Americas; and its rapid fall to the devaluation of the gold and silver coinage which resulted. These passements, often made by men, were worked with large heavy bobbins to maintain the straightness of the thread. The extremely low level of their survival came from the social factors which led to their being unravelled so that the gold could be recovered for financing battles. Pure gold, or gold-plated wire was sometimes used, but more commonly gold foil was beaten very thin and wound in narrow strips around silk, strands of parchment or even paper (fig. 64).

b. Gold lace, metal strips linked by thin bars are used to produce a rich openwork effect, 19th century.

64. a. Heavy bobbins indicate heavy thread. Title page of the Froschauer pattern book, 1561 (courtesy: Zentralbibliothek, Zurich).

### *Silk*

Silk-cultivation was at this time still a bit of a novelty in western Europe. Silk laces are mentioned in an introdcution to the Froschauer pattern book of bobbin laces published in Zurich in 1561[74], and the sixteenth-century silk laces of fashion came mostly from Milan, Genoa and Lucca in northern Italy. Burattos from southern Italy and Sardinia consisted of a silk gauze embroidered with floss in a wide range of colours more subtle than the rainbow – carmine, salmon pink, lemon yellow, azure, ivory, moss green, ochre or tangerine – but they were for hangings or coverlets rather than fashion. The gauzy technique is first mentioned in western literature by Aristotle (384–322 BC). Its near invisibility, which revealed rather than clothed the human form was, as with similar textures of linen and cotton, an object of wonder.

The fashionability of silk and precious metal laces in the later sixteenth century was threatened by sumptuary edicts which limited their wearing to the upper levels of society; by their cost to the country, being imported items; by a reluctant puritanism stemming from the Reformation; and more importantly by the increasing value of fine linen underwear as a status symbol, following improvements in flax cultivation and spinning in the earlier part of the century. As the quality and luxury of woven linens improved, underwear made a natural transition to upperwear, in the form of shirts and shifts which then, being visible, were decorated in the manner of drawnwork and cutwork, in other words embroidered laces. These had already for some time, and in a coarser form, enhanced ecclesiastical and secular furnishings. As textures and embroidery became finer and finer, cutworks became converted into sensational ruffs encircling the nobly privileged necks of royalty and its minions, and the era of lace – linen lace – in fashion had truly began (see fig. 46).

With this new form of decoration, silk could not compete. Silks had been used for blackwork embroidery on linen and this, seen in a painting, is easily mistaken for drawnwork, for which coloured silks were also used, binding residual warps and wefts in strands of crimson, blue or brown to create square meshes with spaced blocks left to form the design (see fig. 65, colour). But for the further transition into punto in aria, the slippery nature of silks made them unsuitable, nor could they be, like linen, easily stiffened to make standing collars or millstone ruffs (fig. 66a). From this time, the popularity of linen laces grew, and silk as the premier fashion thread was passed over.

66b. Frances, Countess of Thanet, wearing a dress banded with black silk bobbin lace, D.Mytens c1620 (courtesy: Christie's, London).

66.a. Princess de Conde, Eleonore de Bourbon, by P.P.Rubens, early 17th century. (photo: Harold Corsini, courtesy: The Frick Art Museum, Pittsburgh, PA). The standing collar of silk gauze is supported by an arc of reticella and punto in aria, itself supported by a wire underpropper or by starch. (see also fig.66c, colour).

Although the production of black silk laces, especially for mourning, or for ageing ladies, never entirely ceased (fig. 66b), silk did not truly reappear in fashion until the mid-eighteenth century, when bobbin laces reasserted themselves as the leading fashion technique, and the French silk blondes leapt suddenly into popularity. From that time on, while not supplanting linen, silk maintained a strong hold. In the late eighteenth century, Chantilly laces of matt silk began; and patent silk nets, made by a weft- or by a warp-knitting technique were successfully marketed. During the Napoleonic wars (1804–15), while the importation of French silk products into England was disallowed, production of silk laces began in the East Midlands, but it was short-lived, failing to survive the re-opening of trade with France.

In the 1830s Maltese lace was revived. Spanish bobbin laces remained predominantly of silk throughout, though they were never truly fashionable outside their country of origin (fig. 67). Their lustrous silks were of two thicknesses, the lighter quality (lower denier) constructing the ground and, in the solid design areas, interweaving with thicker shinier threads (figs. 68a–c). In the 1860s, the entire European silk production was almost annihilated by the disease pébrine which killed off the worms. As the industry gradually recovered, thanks to the detection by Louis Pasteur of the causative germ, exquisitely fine Chantilly shawls reappeared, to die again with the fall of the Second Empire in 1872. Lyons lace, made on the Pusher machines from 1870, used glistening white or black silks imported from China. The more luxurious Russian laces were worked in a mixture of dyed silks and precious metal (see fig. 51). Multi-coloured silks were also used in the needle-knotted laces of Turkey and Armenia (see fig. 41b). As with early metal laces, early silks are rare, their low survival rate resulting in this instance from the use of mordants, to fix the colours, which gradually rotted the fibres.

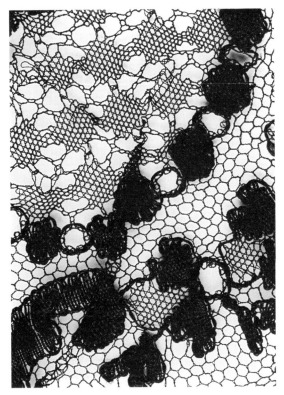

68.a. Chantilly lace, continuous-thread technique, in matt silk dyed black. This large flounce was constructed by joining strips of lace invisibly together.

67. Detail of Spanish blonde (photo John Knight, courtesy W.S.C.A.D.).

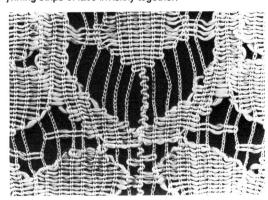

b. Warp-knitting, from a modified Stocking Frame machine.

68d. Chinese silk used for Lyons Pusher-machine laces, from the 1870s.

68c. Maltese lace, a thick lustrous silk the colour of ripening corn.

Silk, and indeed cotton and linen as well, are sometimes described as being 'as fine as gossamer'. But how fine *is* gossamer? This spider silk, not markedly different in chemical composition from the true silk of *Bombyx mori*, may be as miniscule as 1 to 3 microns in diameter[75]. It was natural enough that enthusiastic experimenters should visualize gossamer as a cheap silk substitute: after all, spiders are everywhere. Unfortunately they do not spin fat cocoons with miles of fibre, only webs. They use their silk to snare and enwrap their victims, to swing from one place to another, or to make sticky yellow nests for their numerous eggs. Not only is their silk-supply limited, but they do not take kindly to domestication: in captivity they eat each other in preference to the food provided.

The use of spider silk was nevertheless attempted and a gossamer pair of stockings and gloves was exhibited at the Academy of Science in Paris in 1710[76]. More detail is available of another pair, created in the USA in 1864, the silk being 'milked' directly from the spinnerets of 500 spiders. The stockings were too sheer to wear, and at a price of $100 a pair there was probably little enticement.

Further essays, at the turn of the century, focussed on the two-and-a-half inch long Madagascar spider (*Nephila Madagascariensis*, (see figs. 18c, and 18d colour). Some attempt at farming it was simulated by fencing the spiders into a kind of corral, their heads protruding on one side and their abdomens on the other. Rather like battery hens they were treated as mechanical producers, scarcely able to move or do more than have their gossamer strands reeled from their spinnerets by native girls, until the supply was exhausted and they died.

For the Paris Exhibition of 1900, 25,000 spiders were milked to produce 100,000 yards of 214-strand thread, woven into an 18-yard length of fabric 18 inches wide. But startling as this may sound, it was scarcely likely to incite the commercial exploitation of arachnids as an alternative source of silk. The cost was high, and not only to the spider: 55,000 yards of 19-strand thickness (one strand per spider) weighed only 386 grains, and 7,000 grains were needed to weigh one pound (avoirdupois, equivalent to 16 ounces), valued at that time at $40[77].

### Linen

The earlier linen laces, though of superb quality, were of relatively heavy thread (240 microns in diameter)[78], but towards the end of the seventeenth century they became progressively finer until thread counts of 1,200 (45 microns diameter)[79] were being used for both bobbin and needle laces from Flanders, France and Venice. Some account of the problems of spinning such near-invisible and almost intangible yarn has been given in chapter 6. The most famous spinners were said to be in France, in the area of Valenciennes and Cambrai. Flax from Courtrai was sent there, and the spun yarn passed on to the Netherlands for whitening, before going back to Flanders to be turned in lace.

Very fine hand-spinning continued into the mid-nineteenth century, mainly in Holland and Germany, though by that time it was under increasing competition from finely-spun cottons made on constantly improved machines. An account in the *Illustrated Exhibitor* of 1851 (p.333) speaks of the extreme delicacy of the linen thread used at that time in Brussels laces, though this was probably only for exhibition purposes. It sometimes cost £160 per pound weight, and even then nearly half of it had to be wasted because it was not sufficiently refined. The finest quality is described as 'so extraordinarily tenuous' that it 'cannot be worked when the wind is in the north, or the slightest breathy of air moves . . . Linen thread thus obtained is worth more than six times its weight in pure gold, affording a striking exemplification of the manner in which labour imparts value to raw material'. A single filament was scarcely visible, even when backed by a blue ground. It would take 400 bobbins and three weeks' labour to make a Flemish ell (three-quarters yard) of Mechlin lace three inches wide, which would then cost £10.

Just as linen was difficult to dye, so it was difficult to bleach, at least to the bright brashness so characteristic of chlorine-bleached cottons in the nineteenth century. So it was that linen's pale off-whiteness, of a waxy lustre like the face of a corpse, came to have an important social cachet in the nineteenth-century, while cotton, until it earned its own supremacy, was regarded as cheap and common. However the creamy pallor could go too far, and Brussels linen yarns were sometimes criticized for their slightly jaundiced look, acquired while retting in the 'golden' river Lys[80]. Attempts to correct this by powdering the lace with lead carbonate was a risky practise since in the presence of hydrogen sulphide, produced in small quantities by coal fires, the would-be whitener was converted to a greyish lead sulphide which instead of washing out was only strengthened by immersion in water.

Basically, bleaching involved boiling the linen in potash or other alkali (lye), sometimes with the addition of cow dung[81], then souring it with an acid such as buttermilk to neutralize it, spreading the woven cloth in special fields guarded from thieves by watch towers – and repeating the whole process every few days over a four to five week stretch. Some idea of the extraordinary problems which beset the bleachers of linen cloth in the first half of the eighteenth century is conveyed by *The State of the Linen Manufacture* in Scotland between the years 1728 and 1751. A great deal of capital was laid out in the preparation of a number of bleachfields, but the heavy duties on imported 'Sope, Ashes and other Materials used in Bleaching' made it inordinately expensive and 'led the poor Weavers to use Lime and other noxious Lees which destroyed the ffabric of the Cloth'. Experiments were made in bleaching with Kelp (calcined ashes of seaweed formerly used in making soap), but this gave the linen a yellow tinge. In Scotland, there were 'Trials for making of Ashes, fit for Bleaching, of ffearns [bracken?] a weed that is to be had in great plenty in this Country'. In Ireland, gorse was used to heat the huge pots in which the linen was boiled, and the alkaline ash was then added to the water. By 1734, the Scottish Trustees were using 'their utmost endeavours to come at the secret of the dutch methods of Bleaching. They sent a young man to Holland of purpose to acquire it, who, after continuing there for a considerable time was obliged to come away without it, the dutchmasters having with the greatest secrecy concealed the mystery from him'. The fame of Haarlem may well have derived from the purity of the water, filtered through the surrounding sand dunes, but equally the Dutch success, as that of the Belgian flaxmasters, may have lain in their professionalism. Using organized large-scale cooperative schemes, each stage of this highly skilled work could be handled by experts.

In the late eighteenth century, the use of chloride of lime for bleaching was invented in Glasgow. It did away with all the earlier difficulties but added another: it harmed the linen.

From the late nineteenth century, it was mainly in agricultural communities such as Denmark and central Italy that linen continued to be spun by hand and to be used for bobbin, needle and embroidered laces. But these were for family use, not fashion, and so were no rival to the dominance of 'king cotton'.

During the same period, artistic revivals occurred, including the Ruskin laces of Cumbria. The general quality of these late hand-spun yarns was variable, and the counts low, i.e. the threads were thick. Although excellent yarn could by special effort still be spun, in general the industry of flax

hand-spinning in Belgium was in decay by the mid-1840s, and machine-spinning, slowed by the economic crisis of 1845–8, went ahead again after 1850. But even that failed to progress and soon the raw linen was being sent to England to be spun by machine, and the yarn then returned to Belgium for further manufacture into lace or woven goods[82]. By 1904, Belgium had only 300,000 spindles for flax, compared with a total of 1,130,000 in Ireland, Scotland and England[83].

### Cotton

The very first cotton laces were made on a loom, and called *loom laces*. Gauze weaves, patterned with cats and birds, are known from 1000 AD Peru. The loosely-knotted square trelliswork of Peruvian nets is stabilized by the overtwisted yarn of the decoration which causes irregular lumps and nodules to cling like the rootlets of ivy to their tenuous support, holding it together (figs. 69a,b). Needle-lace loopings have been found in functional, non-lace, cotton socks from the deserts of Arizona, and are thought to date from the eleventh century AD but the technique occurred much earlier in South America, made of plyed yarn, and associated with the wrappings of the dead.

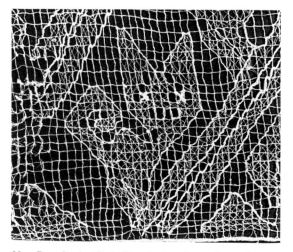

69.a. Peruvian 'netting' with a design of cats diagonally arranged, c1000 AD. Cotton, spun Z plyed S.

However, fashion laces of cotton were strictly a nineteenth- and twentieth- century phenomenon – a fact important to remember when dating laces. Cotton from India had for centuries been woven into breathlessly translucent muslins so light they floated on air like 'webs of woven wind'. These

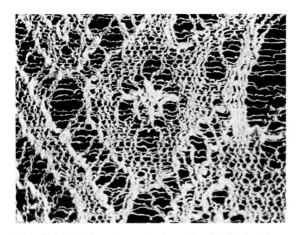

69.b. Detail of a Peruvian gauze lace, showing the boucle effect of overtwisted cotton yarn (both courtesy Museum of Mankind).

cottons reached western Europe from the East Indies by the second half of the seventeenth century. Already by 1678 wool manufacturers were protesting about the increasing use of cotton for children's clothing and for waistcoat linings. In 1696 *The Naked Truth* commented: 'Fashion is truly turned a witch; the dearer and scarcer any commodity, the more the mode. 30s a yard for muslins, and only the shadow of a commodity when procured!'[84] In 1697 nearly 2,000,000 pounds of raw cotton was imported into Great Britain[85], causing such damage to the wool trade that in 1700 the sale of imported cotton goods was prohibited at the urging of the sheep farmers and wool manufacturers. But ladies of fashion loved the challenge and exclusiveness of clandestine goods. The embargo was reinforced in 1712, but was still ineffective, the greatest benefactor being the Dutch East India Company which turned readily to smuggling. In 1721 a fine of £5 on the wearer and £20 on the vendor of cotton goods was imposed[86] – equivalent to at least forty times that amount today.

Interestingly, in spite of the innumerable paeons of praise heaped on the exquisite delicacy, softness and transparency of Dacca muslins, Baines, given a fragment which dated from 1786, commented: 'yet the yarn of which it is woven is not so fine as some which has been spun by machines in this country'[87]. He calculated that one pound weight of the yarn would produce 115 miles, 2 furlongs and 16 yards, equivalent to a count of 240. At that time, 1835, the English machines could spin a 350-count cotton. For weaving into muslin, however, thicker yarns such as 220s to 250s, were used, equating in fact with the India muslin warps. Nevertheless, the India muslins were both softer and more durable.

By 1820, a combination of factors, including the competition from British spinners and weavers, and an increase in the price of cotton, led to a decline in Dacca production. Marsden, writing in 1884 (p.35), gives a 30s count as the finest that could be spun from Indian cotton, while Peruvian could be spun to 70s, Egyptian to 200s, and Sea Island above 200s. A report to the House of Commons on East India cotton on 31 October 1906, included the following statement: 'I am strongly of the opinion that every indigenous Indian variety has degenerated due to exhausted soil, inferior cultivation and the continued use of unselected seed over many generations'.

The use of cotton for embroidered laces dates from the first half of the eighteenth century, when fine muslins were converted in Saxony into exquisitely delicate pulled threadworks, no warps or wefts being removed (see fig. 63). Cotton knitting yarns appear to date from the same period, and by the 1760s openwork knitting by hand, in silk and cotton, was inspiring the first experiments in the manufacture of laces by machine.

The use of cotton for trend-setting bobbin and needle laces came later, waiting on the Industrial Revolution and improvements in spinning machines to produce a yarn of sufficient smoothness and strength at an economic price. The smoothness was essential since both these lace techniques involve a great deal of friction, in bobbin laces in tightening the twists and crosses to control the tension, and in needle laces in constantly pulling the yarn through dozens of loops, one after the other. Any lumpiness would certainly produce a fluffy or irregular effect, and quite probably breakage because of the vacillation of the tensile strength and elongation-to-break factors along the yarn's length.

The stimulus to mechanization was a spin-off from the import restrictions intended to protect the wool trade but in fact backfiring on its protectors since the prohibited importations of woven cottons were converted into importations of raw cotton for home manufacture. Industrialization advanced by leaps and bounds as the eighteenth century rushed by. The increased speed of weaving which resulted from the invention of the Flying Shuttle in 1733 left the looms gasping for yarn. In 1760, the Society of Arts offered a premium for improvements to the spinning wheel and, though it was not awarded, it accelerated experiment, and between 1764 and 1770 Hargreaves invented his Spinning Jenny (i.e. engine), which could keep 16 to 30 spindles active all at the same time, producing a soft lightly twisted yarn basically similar to that of hand-spinning, and not strong. Arkwright's Water Frame, initially powered by horses, but soon afterwards by water, produced a harder yarn known as 'water-twist', converting 1 pound of raw cotton into 19 miles of yarn, equivalent to a 40s count[88]*. By 1798 it could make yarns as fine as 70s (*The Manufacturer's Assistant*). Crompton's Mule, a hybrid of the two earlier machines, could by 1780 spin a stronger more even thread of 60 to 80 count, which sold at 42 shillings a pound (£2 10s)[89]. However, not until 1783 was cotton strong enough to make the warps, formerly provided by linen threads, in addition to the wefts. Only then, could cloth entirely of cotton be manufactured in England. By 1803, cotton could be used for the patent nets of the warp-knitting machines; and in 1809 it was, right from the start, adopted in a doubled form by Heathcoat's newly patented Bobbinet machine[90]. In 1805, Messrs Houldsworth of Manchester were spinning counts of 220 (at £3 3s 6d per lb) and 300 (at £12 8s 6d per lb). By 1812, they could produce 352s at £27 8s per lb, and while the American embargo on the export of raw cotton to Britain between 1807 and 1811 must certainly have delayed experiments in its use for handmade laces, by 1815 Samuel Cartledge of Nottingham had established fine counts of doubled cotton yarn which were acceptable to East Midlands bobbin lacemakers. A little later the use of cotton was extended to Honiton. The defluffing of the yarn by gassing or singeing, combined with improvements in spinning (the invention of the Ring-spinner, and shortly afterwards the Self-acting Mule), made cotton very adequate indeed for hand lacemaking, although the fibre ends never disappear entirely but are constantly regenerated by friction during use, producing a variable fluffiness which can be a method of distinguishing cotton from linen laces.

By 1833 prejudice against the use of cotton had been subdued, if not totally silenced. Protests against it for Alençon needle laces remained heated, as Mme Despierres records. As late as 1857, sorrow was being expressed at the 'reprehensible substitution of cotton which might lead to the ruin of the industry', and some protested they 'would not compromise their reputation for such a minimal economy in raw material' (fig. 70). A Monsieur Lefrou on the other hand wrote in praise of cotton: 'the ease with which it can be worked, the beauty of the lace, the frequent absence of solidity of linen thread, the considerable advances that have been made in the manufacture of cotton thread . . . are all good reasons for its use'. Mme Despierres herself,

70. Alencon needle lace, 19th century. Note the ground of brides tortillees and the difference in thickness between the linen threads of the openwork, and the cotton of the solid design, areas.

writing in 1886, points out that Brussels, Mechlin and Valenciennes laces had all been made in cotton since 1830.

It appears that high counts were early available: the *Manufacturer's Assistant* of 1798 quotes a 220 count of 'India twist' at £104 a pound, with discounts available for quantity. The progression of increasing perfection was undeniably there, at a cost below and a fineness above that of linen, so that it was inevitable that sooner or later cotton yarn would surpass linen and establish itself as the prima donna of lace fashion.

The years between 1785 and 1790 were momentous ones for the cotton industry: chlorine bleach was invented, steam was applied to the spinning machines, and the first importations of Sea Island cotton reached England from South Carolina. The fibres from this species were long, strong, smooth and silky, and could revolutionize the thread. The plants were small, of relatively low yield, delicate enough to be harmed by wind, frost and rain which caused the flowers to drop off so that no bolls were formed, and very vulnerable also to insect pests such as the boll weevil which eventually wiped out the strain in the 1960s – by which time it was in any case no longer economic to spin it.

By the end of the nineteenth century, cotton yarn was so much finer than that currently available in linen that it was universally used for west European fashion laces made by hand. Even the glorious bridal veil created by Leon Sacré of Brussels in the needle-lace point de gaze for the marriage of the Princess Stephanie of Belgium to Prince Rudolph of Austria in 1881 was made of cotton (fig. 71).

Cotton yarns now matched in fineness those made of linen two hundred years before. And yet, between the many copies of Venetian needle laces – made at the turn of the century in Burano, Vienna, Barcelona, Bologna, Belgium, Ireland and Bayeux – and the originals which they imitated, lay a whole world of difference. Even when the stitch densities almost (though never quite) match, the originals are cool, pliant and lustrous; the copies harsh, stiff and dull, marvellously constructed, yet dead. Not that all were comparable: some left everything except cheapness to be desired. Fig. 72a shows a Singapore 'point de Venise' of the 1980s, photographed at the same magnification as fig. 56, but with thread so thick and stitches so large that a single loop will scarcely fit into the frame.

71. A corner of the marriage veil of the Princess Stephanie. Leon Sacre, and Bruxelles 1880, are worked on either side of the central motif (courtesy: Smithsonian Institution).

72.b. Threads as fine: above, handspun linen, needle lace applique on droschel; below, handspun cotton, pulled thread embroidery. Both 18th century.

Note: (a) and (b) are at the same magnification.

72. a. Singapore lace in the style, but not the texture, of 17th century Venetian.

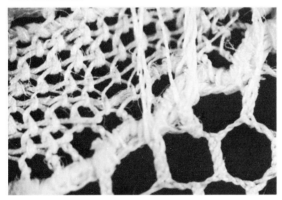

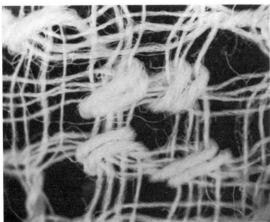

Certainly many of the copies were of cotton fibres which, compared with linen, are shorter, tougher and less reflective. But cotton, lightly hand-spun into delicately fluctuating whispers, and hand-woven into open miracles of translucent muslin has a fascination and beauty which almost matches that of the early linens. These, under the microscope, are a joy to see. Their clear glowing strands, of variable thinness, contribute a spontaneous charm to the lovely designs and superlative textures of the finished piece, drawing the eye with constant delight from one area to another, as the skill of the spinner casts its mystical spell (fig. 72b).

It is *this* vitality, this human element, that is lacking in the copies, stultified by the fixed, unyielding, monotonous regularity of the machine-spun thread, drawn and plyed with implacable speed to a fixed automation of unvarying diameter so that, closely worked, it makes the lace itself look spiritless and inflexible. Even the lace from Vienna (fig. 73a), made of an undistinguished machine-spun linen, appears, when magnified $\times 40$, extraordinarily dull. In its proper contemporary place, machine-spun cotton is more successful. In the bobbin finings of fig. 62b, for example, the bobbin yarns meander in a fluid motion through the sleek warps which lie straight and untwisted down the length of the lace.

Nevertheless, the imitations, made with a dedicated perfectionism, should not be undervalued. They were, in the context of a Europe already highly industrialized, works of art in themselves, and they endowed cotton – linked to the bright frivolity of high and constantly changing fashion – with, at second-hand, all the venerable attributes of antiquity (figs. 73b–g. See also Table 6).

Conditions in the factories were something else. In 1838, one-seventh of the work force was under fourteen years of age, and more than half under sixteen. The Factory Bill of 1833, proposing the reduction of the working day from fourteen hours to ten, was felt to be 'too great and too sudden' a change. 'We are of the opinion,' a representative of the firm of M'Connell and Kennedy, Manchester, continued, 'that 69 hours a week, or say 66, are not too long labour in cotton-spinning factories for children of proper age'. The demand for children under 14 was greater for the finer counts, i.e. above 150. By 1850, 'the yarn spun would, in a single thread, pass 408,000 times around the globe, it would reach 102 times from the earth to the sun, and encircle the earth's orbit 17 times'. It was further estimated that to spin this amount by hand in the same length of time, 80 million spinsters would be needed, in place of the 21 million spindles powered by water and steam which operated in nearly 2,000 factories throughout the kingdom[91].

In the same year, 114 million yards of cotton lace and bobbinet were exported. But while quite favourable reports were given of conditions in the spinning mills, in the lace factories they were not so good. Graphic descriptions at a meeting in Nottingham in 1860 revealed that:

'there was an amount of privation and suffering . . . which was utterly unknown in other towns in this kingdom, or indeed in the civilized world. Many children, nine or ten years old, were engaged from perhaps two, three or four o'clock in the morning until ten, eleven or twelve o'clock at night, and indeed sometimes later . . . The Nottingham trade had for some time past been suffering from the effects of the prevailing fashions, comparatively little lace being now worn.' The speaker thought that 'if this fact were made known to Her Majesty she would (as in the case of Coventry, where the riband trade was so depressed), bring lace again into fashion'. (*Times* Jan. 16, 1860).

Mercerized cottons are still normal cotton but, from the point of view of practical textile products, improved in strength and appearance. However their excessive whiteness was felt, at the turn of the century, to be a disadvantage, for the tints of antique laces had again risen to the heights of social advantage. Indeed 'white lace' in the mid-century tended to be a derogatory term implying machine-made, cotton and common. The whiteness was therefore concealed beneath dyes giving creamy tints of beige, butter or écru.

73c. From the Aemilia Ars Society of Bologna, arms of the Volta-Campeggi family, after a 16th-century design by Passarotti.

73. Early laces and copies:
a. (i) A collar from the Imperial Central School of Lacemaking in Vienna c1900 (photo John Knight, courtesy: W.S.C.A.D.);

(ii) detail (magnification as fig.56).

b. Imitation of 17th century Venetian, probably made in France c1880.

73d. Argentan, a rochet made by the firm of Lefebure for
the Jubilee of Pope Leo XIII in 1887.

e. Punto in aria, c1610.

NB. a(ii), e, and f, magnification as fig.56.

f. Cyprus reticella, 20th century.

g. Another example of Youghal, showing a strong Z ply
linked with an S closure (top left). Note the extreme
mechanical regularity of diameter of the cotton thread.

Table 6.

## YARN AND FIBRE DIAMETERS C1600 TO 1900, ARRANGED CHRONOLOGICALLY

| LACE | DATE | FIBRE | THREAD DIAMETER | FIBRES PER THREAD | SPIN/PLY | TWISTS PER MM. | STITCHES PER MM. |
|---|---|---|---|---|---|---|---|
| Reticella (needle) | c1600 | Linen | 250 - 400 microns (may be up to 500) | | 2 Z plyed S | 4 | S-closure 2 stitches per mm. |
| Punto in aria (needle) Fig.73e | c1610 | Linen | 120 - 140 microns | | Z plyed S | 4 (unused thread) 1.75 (looped area) | Z closure 2 per mm. |
| Flemish collar (bobbin lace) | c1625 | Linen | 240 - 250 microns | | S-ply. Spin appears mildly Z or S, or dead straight | 2 (final effect almost straight) | |
| Valenciennes (bobbin lace) | c1700 | Linen | 30-40 microns also up to 105 microns in same clothstitch area | 12 per 40 micron thread (fibre diam. 11.5 ) 20 per 66 micron thread | 2-Z plyed S | 16 | |
| Binche (bobbin lace) | Early 18thC | Linen | 45-105 microns in same area. Some 35. | | ? S singles. Partially untwisted 2-S plyed S | 10 | |
| Venetian gros point (needle) | c1650 -1700 | Linen | 50 - 70 microns | 16 - 28 (12.5-13.2 microns diameter) | S (singles?) | 7 | S-closure 5.5 - 6.0 (close form) |
| Venetian coralline (needle) | c1700 | Linen | 130 - 140 microns | 36 - 51 21 microns diam - 19.6 microns | S plyed S or very weak Z plyed S | 3 (unworked) | S-closure 3 (close form) |
| Point d'Angleterre | c1730 | Linen | 60 - 70 microns | 22 (12.8 microns diameter) | S singles | 6 (fairly tight) | bobbin lace |

| | | | | | | | |
|---|---|---|---|---|---|---|---|
| Muslin (woven) | early 18th C | Cotton | 110 microns 40 - 50 microns | not counted 10-11 (12.6 microns) | Z singles | 3 18 | Z-closure 6.5 stitches/mm. |
| Reseau Venise (needle) | 1st half 18th C | Linen | 35-40 microns in solid areas, 70 in ground | 14 to 18 9.4 microns diam. | tight S singles | 26 (up to 40 in straight return threads) | 5.5stitches/mm. |
| Alencon (needle) | 2nd half 18th C | Linen | min. 30 microns but variable | ? 12 ? 9 microns diam. | S singles | 35 | Z-closure 3 st/mm. (open - typical of Flanders) |
| Flemish mixed needledesign bobbinground | c1750 | Linen (fig.73f) | 35 microns finest | 8 (12.4 diameter) | S singles | ? 37 | |
| Needle applique on bobbinground (droschel) | late 18thC | Linen | Needle: 70 Bobbin : 40 attaching thread:30 | 18 (16.5 diam.) 19-23 | S S singles | 11 8.9 | Z-closure 2 st./mm (needle) |
| Youghal (needle) | c1890 | Cotton | 90 - 110 microns | numerous | Unused: 2Z plyed S In stitches: Z almost unwound | 10 | S-closure 3 st./mm. |
| Imitation 17thC Venetian gros point (French?) | c1880 | Linen (fig.56x) | 160 Appears hairy and crushed by vigorous rubbing | No loose ends for accurate (dull) | weakly Z plyed S | 2 | S-closure 2.25 st./mm. |
| Burano copy of 17thC | c1900 | Cotton (brown) | 200 microns | | 2S plyed S | 6 - 8 | S-closure 3 st./mm. |

| Sample | Date | Material | Thread diameter | Fibre diameter | Ply / twist | | Closure / stitches |
|---|---|---|---|---|---|---|---|
| Vienna copy of 17thC Venetian | c1900 | Linen machine-spun (no lustre) | 100 microns | | 2 S plyed Z | 8 | 4.5 Z-closure (needle) |
| Ruskin (needle) | c1900 | Cotton/linen mix | 500 microns | (threads too thick to focus) | 2 Z plyed S | 2 | S-closure 1.5 st./mm. |
| Point de gaze (needle) | c1900 | Cotton | Ground 45 microns Design areas 50-90. Individual threads constant | 18 - 21 (10.6 microns diam.) | S (2-ply, but first spin unwound. fibres straight | 10 | Z-closure 4.25 st./mm. (open form) |
| Leavers (Bobbin fining) | c1912 | Cotton and rayon | Brass bobbins 65. Rayon warps unspun | 20 - 25 (Cotton 14.5 microns) | | 6.67 | (machine) |
| Belgian point de Venise (needle) | c1930 | Cotton | 130 - 190 microns | ? 33 (22.6 diam.) | S | 7 | Z-closure 2.5 st./mm/ |
| Cyprus (reticella) (needle) | 20th C | Cotton (Fig.73g) | 350 microns | could not count (15 micron diam?) | Weak S plyed Z | 3 | S-closure 1/mm. |
| Singapore 'point de Venise' (needle) | 1980s | Cotton | 500 microns | could not count Fibres 18 - 20 microns diam | 3 Z plyed S | 3.5 - 4 | S-closure 1.5 st./mm. |

THIS TABLE IS BASICALLY A COMPARISON OF 16TH-CENTURY LINEN WITH 19TH TO 20-CENTURY COTTON LACES

Note: Handspun threads vary considerably (a) in diameter along their length: (b) according to how much the lacemaking process has changed them.

From the point of view of textiles in general, wool is of prime importance. For lace, however, the scaliness and elasticity of its fibres make it difficult to use, as well as limiting the appeal of the finished article. It had some fashionability, from the sixteenth century onwards, for rustic wear, burials, and furnishing, but almost never as a part of fashion in its true sense. Indeed in the seventeenth century it was felt politic to promote the use of woollen lace by the Burial in Woollen Acts of 1667 and 1678. In connection with these, Charles II granted a monopoly for the making of woollen laces 'for the burial of the dead or otherwise' to Amy Potter of St Paul's Churchyard (patent no. 204). In those times of high mortality, interments were an important source of wealth, providing a sink for the British wool trade, still a vital keystone of the economy.

· The further aim of the Acts was to slow down the importations of fine linen fabrics and laces from the Netherlands and Flanders – which everyone desired. Imports were far exceeding exports, and the balance of payments had taken a disquietingly downward turn. The Acts were, however, pitifully ineffective, and feelings ran high. Mr Francis Jenks, speaking in the Common Hall on the 24th of June 1679, blamed the 'poverty and ruine' of the City on the French,

> 'who have laid such great Impositions upon our Woollen cloth that we have almost lost our Trade with France; they have spoild out Trade with Holland, Flanders and Germany, by a destructive War; they have beggared many thousands of our honest and industrious Weavers by the vast quantity of their Silks, and other unnecessary Commodities imported hither: so that upon an exact balance of the Trade between us and them taken, this Kingdom doth lose Eleven hundred thousand pounds every year'.

The nature of Amy Potter's lace is unknown, except that it would have been bobbin-made, and that it resembled the French Colbertine. The Acts remained on the Statute book for the next 120 years, and the recoiling horror of socialites at the thought of wearing wool, even for burial – or perhaps of *not* wearing linen with its long history of religious symbolism and association with Pharoahs, Emperors and Kings – are expressed vividly in Pope's *Epistle to a Lady*, written in 1735:

> 'Odious! in woollen! 'twould a saint provoke!
> (Were the last words that poor Narcissa spoke).
> No, let a charming chintz and Brussels lace
> Wrap my cold limbs, and shade my lifeless face'.

It remained for the nineteenth century to make some more attractive use of wool. From the 1820s, misty handspun singles were knitted into Shetland marriage shawls, so light that a six-foot square weighed only a quarter of an ounce[92] and could be drawn through a wedding ring. Yak laces of the East Midlands were bobbin-made in a geometry of thread movements enlivened by earthy colours, their firm yarns derived from English worsteds, not from Tibet (see fig. 23). They were used mostly for trimming winter skirts, cloaks or christening capes, around the 1870s, after Dr Jaeger had proselytized the link between Wool and Health. However, the comparative lightness of wool meant that it draped less well than either silk or linen. Its relative lack of lustre made it appear dull. Its tendency to shrink and felt when washed meant that the display of design soon lost its crispness – indeed it was always limited – while the tendency of the fibres to fluff out from the yarn, then to cling together in bobbles or neps, did not increase its attractiveness. Wool did not stiffen up well with starch. It was tempting to insect appetites, both clothes moth and carpet beetle, and woollen lace stored from one season to the next was likely to be resurrected with far more holes in it than the lacemaker ever intended, or indeed than was good for its stability.

In Iceland, sheep remain clothed in their ancestral form, with a double coat. The shaggy outer hair, covered with small close scales, nor unlike a goat's, can be cleaned to a lustre which makes it look like silk, then dyed red and green and worked into traditional lace styles for the trimming of the bodice and skirts of provincial dress.

Certain types of mammalian hair developed a snob value. Mohair yarn was finer than worsted, it wore well (had good abrasion resistance) and shone with an attractive gloss. Added to silk, it gave additional warmth and body without detracting from its sheen. This mixture, or pure mohair, was used by the firm of Dognin in Lyons for the manufacture of large shawls made on the Pusher machine, and marketed as 'lama' (fig. 74) during the crinoline period.

While it is extremely unlikely that pure cashmere was ever used for lace – where its expensive qualities of warmth, softness and fineness would be largely wasted – its name was applied to creamy worsteds in the 1860s, making them sound desirable as *cashmère en nuance crème*. The fibre diameter of cashmere is a tiny 13 microns compared with the best Merino at 18 microns or more. However, its high price, added to the extended cost of lacemaking when paid at any

74. Detail of a Pusher machine 'lama' shawl, made of mohair, probably by the firm of Dognin in Lyons.

kind of a living wage, would give it no commercial advantage whatsoever over the more practical fibres of linen, cotton and silk.

In theory there is no reason why any mammalian hair – cat, dog, rabbit etc should not be used. The limitations are purely practical, concerning the amount available, the ease of culling and preparation, and the length of the fibres which largely determines both their adherence during the spin and the shagginess or otherwise of the final product. However in the absence of the more suitable threads, the ingenuity of lacemakers has been known to overcome such difficulties.

*Pig bristles* for example have been used for bobbin laces in the rural Queyras area of southeastern France, 2,000 metres up, near the border with Switzerland[93]. The laces were made without prickings, using a vertically-mounted drum-shaped revolving pillow (or tambour), so that considerable yardages could be produced without the necessity for repositioning the lace (fig. 75, colour).

Neither pig bristles, horsehair nor human hair have any strong link with fashion. Nor are the rare and one-off usages of bast fibres particularly relevant: lace bark is extracted from the outer layers of the Jamaican *Lagetta lintearia*, in the form of a meshwork like a ready-made but irregular net (fig. 76, colour). A dress of it was reputedly given to Queen Victoria.

### Man-made threads

The twentieth century has seen the extinction of handmade lace in high and even general fashion. The cost is far too great, and the machines can produce much more dramatic effects which, con-tinuing the nineteenth-century trend towards visual obviousness, is what the public appears to want.

As a pastime, working with synthetics has scarcely been welcomed for hand lacemaking. However since the future of fashion laces undoubtedly rests with the machine, and their popularity with easy-care, neither regenerated nor synthetic fibres can any longer be denied their place. The extremely rapid warp-knitting Raschel machines can produce dress-lengths, yardages, and shaped pieces at very economic prices. Although they cannot use natural fibres because of the excessive linting which clogs the needles with fluff, synthetics themselves are moving in the direction of natural yarn simulation, by the endless extruded filaments being formed into staples, which can then be spun like cotton, to produce softer laces which drape more attractively, and are more moisture absorbent – an important feature where lacy-knit underwear is concerned. In a competitive commercial market, cost as ever is strongly relevant: synthetics are cheaper to produce and easier to handle than cotton yarns, they do not fluff out under the stresses of machine production, their tensile strength is greater, they do not stretch or shrink, and they can be made with great lightness. Forms such as the trilobal polyesters are intended to have a high lustre, though for wedding veils delustering processes using titanium dioxide may be needed to reduce the glare.

*Calcium alginate* is sometimes used on the other currently dominant machine, the Schiffli, which makes laces by embroidering onto disposable fabrics or onto net. When the work is complete, the alginate support is dissolved in water, leaving a lace of guipure form (fig. 77). Alginate may also be used on knitting machines to provide bulk for yarns too fine for the machine to cope with. When the garment is finished, the alginate is easily washed out, leaving a cobwebby fabric.

Acetates (cellulose acetate) may alternatively be used as a backing support by the Schiffli, and then dissolved in acetone. The lace produced is variously known as guipure, chemical or burnt-out, from the corrosive nature of the original process (caustic soda or chlorine being used to destroy a silk foundation).

On other lace machines, such as the Leavers, the alginate can now be used to support the loops or picots. These were a popular feature in early twentieth-century laces, when labour was still cheap, but at that time the supporting strands had to be withdrawn by hand and, with the increase in overheads and labour costs, picots were discontinued, along with large-repeat patterns of an elaborate nature, and the manufacture of very fine threads.

77. A chemical lace, sometimes called Swiss guipure. It consists of embroidery stitches only, worked by interacting needle and shuttle threads, the degradable backing fabric being later removed.

---

*Caution is needed with regard to early records of counts. Marsden (p.329) defines water-twist and mule-yarn counts as the number of 840 yd hanks per lb. *Troy* (i.e. per 12 ounces instead of 16). An 80s Troy would be equivalent to 170s *avoirdupois*.

# 11 Adapting to the present

Lace is a slender openwork fabric made of threads.

Or is it?

While the very essence of lace, its *openwork*, cannot be eliminated, it can be replaced by large holes randomly scattered, which is not precisely the same thing. Modern laces may be far from *slender*, and may even be huge, such as Robin Lewis' torchon hangings (fig. 78), the Kliot's gigantic spread at Berkeley University campus, or Elena Holéczyova's wall hangings made of jute and big enough to cover an interior wall.

As exhibitions of contemporary lace have amply demonstrated, the concept of a *fabric* may be replaced by that of a free-standing three-dimensional form with all the complex angularity of an abstract sculpture.

Even *threads* in their normal sense may be dispensed with: wires, metal strips or other non-spun materials taking over as the manipulative units.

So why do we still call them lace?

The official English definition places no limitation on the *techniques* that must be used, in fact the existence of techniques is scarcely mentioned. Yet in many recent creations from all over the world, it is the use of lace techniques alone – looping, twisting, crossing, knotting – which qualify a particular concept as a lace.

These innovative sculptural or pictorial art forms, using lace techniques, represent one direction in which lace is moving. But there is no reason why this direction should exclude any other. Traditional handmade laces long ago came to a parting of the ways, with the development of 'new' home crafts (tape-based laces, tatting, knitting, crochet etc) in the mid-nineteenth century; new designs (art nouveau bobbin and needle laces *c*1900); and new materials (man-made and synthetic fibres mostly dating from after 1940); while the lace machines introduced an entire new world of skills and techniques from the 1760s onwards.

Rocketing labour costs, annihilated the commercial possibility of truly painstaking production,

78. *Changing Seasons* by Robin Lewis (Mineral Bluff, Georgia), 1980s. One of three panels, 8ft wide by 32ft long, commissioned by the Tennessee Valley Authority for their six-storey atrium in Chattanooga. Torchon technique made to scale using 56 pairs of threads, each five-eighths inch thick, polyester core wrapped in wool/rayon fibre blend, dyed various tints. Each gimp was made of 12 quarter-inch thick threads, untwisted.

whether of thread or lace. Concurrently, a redistribution of wealth decimated the number of consumers who could afford to indulge their vanity or aesthetic whims in the purchase of exquisitely fine fabrics.

Linked with this redistribution was the increasing number of people with a little money to spare, and perhaps a competitive urge to acquire some middle class symbols. This opened the European door to a flood of inexpensive yet good laces from impoverished countries where labour was still extremely cheap, such as China, Brazil and the Philippines. Inevitably, over the decades, the quality of these, too, has slowly deteriorated as the living standards of the natives improved.

There remain the traditionalists, preserving the stitches, designs and constructional features of old laces, but constantly hampered by a shortage of fine threads: the fabulous linen laces of Flanders and the exquisite Venetian productions – dating from the late seventeenth or early eighteenth centuries – making present-day productions appear, under magnification, as if composed of string. But modern threads cannot ever be so slender as before: the flax and cotton varieties which produced them no longer exist. Even if these could be genetically selected and cultivated once more, every stage of their production from sowing to spinning would need to be done by hand; or, if by machine, as were the 420s cottons of 1911, a truly vast order for them would need to be guaranteed before the huge capital outlay could even be contemplated, and that is assuming the machines were available and that the machinists could acquire the highly specialized skill that would be required. We should never forget that fine threads were always priced at several times the value of equivalent weights of silver or gold.

Relics of no. 300 Egyptian cotton may still be jealously hoarded by convents and lace schools, in Kuskinhalas and Argentan for example, which had the foresight to buy in bulk while the yarns were still available, several decades age. However, making lace from them is likely to take hundreds, even thousands, of hours, for quite small pieces, and the three weeks quoted earlier, for three-quarters of a yard of Mechlin lace, probably relates to professionals working at top speed through extremely long days.

For laces of the present and the future, the possibilities still remain fairly wide open. Formerly there were three hand-lacemaking pathways:
1. Prime quality fashion laces, which were commercial and very expensive;

2. Ecclesiastical laces made for the church by non-professionals, and variable in quality;
3. Peasant laces worked in heavy thread, often using home-grown and hand-spun linen, for domestic use.

The first pathway has come to a dead end. The second does not really concern us. But the third can be adapted for useful, attractive trimmings which can be colourful, small, quickly made and still satisfying to produce and effective to wear. Linen threads of a fairly low count, such as 35/3S or 25/2 are best. It is worth bearing in mind that similar heavy threads were used for the very beautiful bobbin laces of Flanders during the first half of the seventeenth century. The patterns for Venetian bobbin laces, printed in *Le Pompe*, or the Swiss passements of 1561 reproduced in *Fascinating Bobbin Lace*, could well be copied perhaps combining, experimentally, a novelty of colour and material with a timelessness of design and long established techniques (fig. 79).

79. Patterns from *Le Pompe*, Venice, 1557; and from a pattern book published by Froschauer in Zurich in 1561. Some of the Zurich laces probably date back to 1536, or earlier.

Other pathways are also available:
4. Hand traditional. Every type of past lace can be copied in stitch, design and technique, although the size and the threads may need to be modified;
5. Hand innovative. Though pleasure may be the prime aim and the only reward of many such laces,

exceptional creations, whether fine or weighty, will probably continue to be commissioned at a satisfactory fee by business premises (for their status value), by museums of modern art (for their originality) or by private patrons (for the enjoyment of looking at them) (fig. 80, colour).

6. Hand commercial.   Laces of all techniques can be made for the open market provided they do not cost too much either in materials or labour. Crochet, bobbin and needle laces made in the East have all appeared in western countries, filling the gaps in the lace supply needed to satisfy tourist demand.

7. Machine laces.   While hand lacemaking is often divorced from any need to earn a living, manufacturers must work for profit, or go out of business. This consideration alone will determine what they are able to produce. Setting-up is expensive, and fineness of thread or complexity of pattern multiply the costs of production in an almost geometric progression (fig. 81). The machine's efforts can however combine art with practicality, given sufficient demand, so that while today good lacemaking by hand is likely to remain extremely limited in extent, the machines can and should supply bulk-demand rapidly and efficiently, and even special orders or short runs of exceptional quality, if the price is right.

It would be foolish to imagine that the lace past can ever be recaptured in its entirety, however hard we may try. But many lacemaking possibilities remain, and we would do well to enjoy them within the limitations of the thread, and time, available.

81.  An intricate pattern demonstrating the industrial advances of railways, electricity and hot air balloons, at the turn of the century.  Made in Calais on the Leavers machine, for the Paris Expo of 1900 (courtesy: Metropolitan Museum of Art, New York).  Such complexity, such fine thread, and such a large repeat, could not even be contemplated today.

*Bast fibres*  Long fibres made of many tiny cells (ultimates) joined end to end, and lying in bundles in the outer layers of the stem. They often have a lignin (wood) content: flax has only 2%.

*Balanced yarns or threads*  The outer and inner stresses of the fibres, resulting from the corkscrew-like contortions they have undergone during the spin (and ply), are matched against each other so that the yarn or thread can hang in a loop without twisting upon itself, or kinking.

*Beetling*  Linen is beaten with wooden blocks to flatten the yarn. The smoother surface reflects more light, improving the lustre. In laces this 'glossing' is performed with small-scale implements such as the aficot.

*Bicomponents*  Double synthetic yarns welded together so that in cross-section they appear bi-lobed. Usually but not necessarily the components are of a different nature.

*Bouclé*  The outer surface of the thread presents a looped appearance, due to controlled over-spinning.

*Braiding, plaiting*  The diagonal interlacing in a fixed order of three or more originally parallel strands.

*Braking*  Beating the flax stems to crush and split them, prior to scutching.

*Carding*  A process preparatory to spinning by which short unwanted fibres are removed and the remaining longer ones partially aligned to form a sliver.

*Combing*  A more refined method of lining up the fibres in parallel, prior to spinning. It follows carding, but is used only for the production of high quality yarns.

*Count*  The comparative thickness of staple yarns and threads expressed as length (in hanks) per fixed weight (one pound).

*Degree of polymerization (D.P.)*  The length of the polymer, or the number of repeat-molecules it contains. The higher the D.P. the stronger the fibre.

*Denier*  The comparative thickness of filament yarns, threads and fibres, expressed as weight (in grams) per fixed length (9,000 metres).

*Density*  Mass per unit volume, measured in grams per cubic centimetre.

*Doubling*  See *Twisting*.

*Drawing, drafting*  The movement of gently pulling small groups of fibres outwards from the rove until they are sufficiently narrowed to be rotated together and fixed in position by the spin.

*Felt*  A fabric made without spinning or weaving. The constituent fibres, e.g. goats' hair or sheep's wool, are made to bond together by intense and prolonged pressure.

*Fibres*  Long thin units, either naturally occurring or made by man, which are put together, usually by spinning, to make yarns and threads.

*Filaments*  Fibres long enough to be measured in yards or even miles (metres or kilometers).

*Flyer*  (a)  An attachment to a spinning wheel, or a spinning machine (e.g. the Water Frame or the Throstle) by which the yarn can be wound on as it is spun, so that the whole process is continuous instead of intermittent.

(b)  An alternative name for the improved Throstle spinning machine, introduced in the late nineteenth century.

*Folding*  See *Twisting*.

*Gauze*  Usually a method of weaving in which the odd-numbered warps are crossed over the even-numbered warps, and held in that position by the weft passage. The term may also be applied to plain weaves in which the yarns are widely spaced.

*Ginning*  The removal of the cotton fibres from the seed.

*Grain*  The smallest unit of English and USA weight, being 1/5,760th pound (Troy) or 1/7,000th pound (avoirdupois). Originally (1542) the weight of a grain of wheat, dry, and gathered from the centre of the ear. Threads of cotton and linen were formerly measured in grains.

*Hackling*    The scutched flax bundles are combed from end to end to remove any unwanted tissues. At the same time they are divided up and brought more or less into line with each other.

*Hard fibres*    Long straight leaf fibres which are embedded in lignin (wood).

*Hard spin*    Fibres tightly spun together to make a yarn, with a high number of turns per inch.

*Hard twist*    Tightly plyed yarns, with a high t.p.i., usually twisted in the same direction as the first spin.

*Linters*    Cotton fibres too short for spinning, and often used for regenerated cellulose (rayon and acetate).

*Looping*    Movements of a single thread, by the hands or with a hook or needle, to form a sequence of interlocking loops which are built up into a fabric.

*Lustre*    The shine of the yarn resulting from its even reflection of light. The lustre of spun threads is directly proportional to the straightness of their component fibres. The lustre of linen is reduced by removal of wax (e.g. by chemical bleaching). It is increased by beetling (smoothing and compressing the fibres in the finished lace). Lustre is reduced by any unevenness of the fibre surface (e.g. by convolutions in cotton, scales in wool, lumps of seracin in silk). Mercerization increases the lustre of cotton.

*Micron*    One-thousandth of a millimetre, often written $\mu$ or $\mu$m (pronounced mew). 1 micron = 1/25,400th inch.

*Molecules*    The basic structural units of a chemical compound, e.g. $H_2O$ (water).

*Muslin*    A soft fine plain-weave cloth of very lightweight construction with the warps and wefts spaced out, which makes it translucent. Usually, though not necessarily, made of cotton.

*Netting*    The manipulation of a single thread using a gauge and a narrow shuttle to produce a fabric of square or diamond-shaped meshes knotted at each corner.

*Plying*    See *Twisting*.

*Polymer*    A macro- (or very large) molecule made up of smaller molecules all of the same type joined together like the links of a chain. To make useful fibres, the polymers must lie straight. The polymer

structure of proteins and cellulose was not confirmed until the 1930s.

*Raw silk*    Silk yarn with the gum (seracin) still in it.

*Reeling*    Winding silk filaments, up to five at a time, directly from the cocoons on to a wheel.

*Rolag*    See *Sliver*.

*Roving*    (a)    verb: The sliver is little by little drawn out by the spinner until it is only one-quarter or one-eighth of its original width. It may be slightly rotated into a cylinder to hold it together. Equivalent to drawing-out in hand spinning.

(b)    noun: The attenuated sliver used in the final stages of spinning.

*Scutching*    The separation on the usable fibres of the retted flax stalk from both the outer rind and the inner wood.

*Singles*    The product of the first spin, or a yarn produced when the fibres are spiralled by the first or single spin.

*Sliver, rove, roving, rolag*    A fairly thin strand of more or less straight and untwisted fibres, produced by carding.

*Soft fibres*    See *Bast fibres*.

*Soft spin*    Fibres lightly spun together to make a yarn with a low number of turns per inch, e.g. from the Spinning Jenny.

*Soft twist*    Lightly plyed yarns with a low t.p.i., or twisted in the reverse direction to the first spin.

*Specific gravity*    The density of a substance in comparison with water, taken as 1, e.g. linen is 1.5 times as heavy.

*Spindle*    A thin stick or similar object which is twirled to reinforce the spin introduced into the drawn-out fibres by movements of the spinner's fingers. In addition, the newly-spun yarn is usually wound on to it.

*Spinning*    (a)    The rotation of short overlapping fibres (staples) around each other tightly enough to make them hold together into a yarn (single), almost infinitely long.

(b)    In man-made fibres and synthetics, the process of forcing liquids through fine holes (spinnerets) to form the fibres. Used similarly of silk-worms and spiders.

*Spinning quality, cohesiveness*    The ease with which fibres both draw out and cling together during spinning.

*Spun silk, waste silk*   Yarns made not by throwing long silk filaments but by spinning shorter broken or damaged pieces which would otherwise be wasted.

*Staples*   Fibres short enough to be measured in inches or centimetres.

*S-spin*   The fibres are rotated so that the slant of their spiralling appears in the yarn like the centre stroke of a letter S.

*S-twist*   Two or more yarns (singles) are twisted (plyed) together in a direction which appears in the thread like the centre stroke of the letter S.

*Tex*   A metric system for expressing the weight/length relationship of fibres, slivers, yarns and threads, intended for universal use, and expressed as the weight in grams of 1,000 metres.

*Textile*   Traditionally, a cloth woven from spun fibres.

*Thread*   The product of a second spin or ply when two or more yarns are twisted together in the same or the reverse direction to the singles. In common usage thread and yarn are interchangeable terms.

*Thread count*   The number of warps per unit width, or weft per unit length, of the fabric.

*Throwing*   Twisting two or more reeled silk filaments together to make a yarn, or two or more yarns together to make a thread.

*Trilobal*   A synthetic fibre which is not circular but has three lobes in cross-section.

*Tussah, wild silk*   Produced by species of moth other than *Bombyx mori*. Wild silk is coarser, less even and darker in colour.

*Twist*   (a)   An alternative name for a plyed yarn, or thread.
(b)   A thread spun clockwise or to the right (Z) with a hard twist, and used in weaving for the warps (Carter).

(c)   In bobbin laces, the right to left movement of the outer threads of two pairs over the inner threads of the same two pairs, making a Z-like stroke (see fig. 50).

*Twisting, doubling, folding, plying*   Two or more yarns are twisted together, either in the same direction as, or reverse direction to, the first spin, to make a thread.

*Ultimates*   The individual cells which, joined end to end and side to side, in small bundles, make up the bast fibres.

*Unbalanced yarns* are usually overtwisted so that the tensions in the outer fibres are too high. During use they tend to unwind and then retwist in the reverse direction.

*Warps*   The numerous longitudinally stretched threads across which the single weft is carried in an over-under (weaving) manner.

*Weft*   The normally single yarn which, passing horizontally, interweaves with the warps. It is usually soft-spun (few turns) in an S direction.

*Whorl*   In hand spinning, a weight, the nature of which is unimportant, attached to the spindle to increase the pull on the yarn as it is spun. When the spindle is light, the whorl provides additional momentum.

*Worsted*   Smooth-surfaced yarns spun from combed wool fibres of narrow diameter.

*Z-spin*   The fibres are rotated so that the slant of their spiralling appears in the yarn like the centre stroke of the letter Z.

*Z-twist*   Two or more yarns are twisted (plyed) together so that their direction appears in the thread like the centre stroke of the letter Z.

# NOTES

1   Andersen and Jørgensen pp. 8–9.
2   Newberry, Introduction.
3   Hall, R. p. 9.
4   Crowfoot p. 38.
5   Baines pp. 57–9.
6   English p. 32.
7   Mitchell pp. 77–8.
8   Ryder pp. 117–132.
9   Exodus 26.
10  Cook p. 80.
11  Wakefield p. 17.
12  Picken p. 67.
13  McIntyre p. 2.
14  *Encyc. Brit.* 1911, 'Gold' p. 201.
15  McIntyre p. 25.
16  McIntyre.
17  Smith and Block p. 53.
18  *Lace and Lacemaking* p. 24.
19  Matthews p. 891.
20  Bussagli pl.XIII.
21  Ryder p. 117.
22  *Identification of Textile Materials*, Table B1.1.
23  Hall, R. p. 10.
24  *Encyc. Brit.* 1911 'Wool' p. 807.
25  Nordland pp. 93–4.
26  Cook p. 22.
27  Cook p. 17, Matthews p. 2.
28  Anton p. 13.
29  Nordland p. 133.
30  Carter p. 174, Pringle *Spinning* p. 45.
31  Kent p. 476.

32  CIBA no. 28.
33  *Everyman's Enc.* 1912, 'Spinning' p. 395.
34  Ashworth p. 12.
35  Welters p. 26.
36  Ashworth.
37  Promotional leaflet from Manila, 1940s.
38  Crowfoot p. 38.
39  Baines p. 5.
40  Wakefield p. 8.
41  Wakefield p. 61.
42  Bellinger p. 23.
43  Vale p. 82.
44  Wakefield p. 55.
45  Jørgensen p. 348.
46  Ashworth.
47  Matthews p. 90.
48  *Everyman* 'Gold' p. 584.
49  Despierres pp. 51–2.
50  Mitchell p. 71.
51  Text Inst. *Id.* p. 247.
52  Kent p. 650.
53  Sonday pp. 62, 67.
54  Sonday p. 71.
55  Wakefield p. 103.
56  Carter 'Rope, Twine and Thread making' p. 99.
57  *ibid.* p. 101.
58  Pringle *Spinning* p. 45.
59  Adburgham p. 10.
60  Anton p. 7.
61  Matthews p. 823.

62  Matthews pp. 834, 837.
63  *Textile Educator* p. 622.
64  Simon.
65  Text. Inst. *Id.* p. 245.
66  von Henneberg p. 76a.
67  Garner p. 86.
68  *US Cotton Fiber Chart*, 1988.
69  Oliver p. 85.
70  Wakefield (1916) pp. 42–3.
71  *ibid.* pp. 4–5.
72  *Textile Educator* p. 662.
73  Wakefield (1916) pp. 11–12.
74  Burkhard.
75  *Enc. Brit.* 'Spider' p. 216.
76  Cook p. 157.
77  Matthews pp. 262–3.
78  Earnshaw p. 89.
79  von Henneberg p. 76a.
80  Carter p. 14.
81  Wily pp. 51–2.
82  Sabbe pp. 78–88.
83  Carter p. 10.
84  Quoted by Crawford, M.
85  *Illust. Ex.* 1852, p. 163.
86  Crawford, M de C.
87  Baines p. 59.
88  Ashworth.
89  Vale p. 95.
90  Felkin p. 169.
91  Lee pp. 128, 130, 173.
92  *Timeless Textiles*, no. 67.
93  Brulet pp. 12–13.

Adburgham, Alison   *Shops and Shopping, 1800-1914*. Allen and Unwin, 1964.

Anderson, S.H. and Jørgensen, Lise Bender   'Ancient Cloth'. *Skalk* no. 1, 1985 (translated by Karen Finch).

Anton, Ferdinand.   *Ancient Peruvian Textiles*. Thames and Hudson, 1987.

Ashworth, Henry   *Historical Data relating to South Lancashire and the Cotton Manufacture*. Manchester, 1866.

Baines, Sir Edward   *History of the Cotton Manufacture in Great Britain*. Cass, 1966 reprint of 1835 ed.

Bellinger, Louisa   *Threads of History*. American Federation of Arts, 1965.

Bird, Junius and Mahler, Joy   'America's Oldest Cotton Fabrics'. *American Fabrics*, no. 20, pp. 73-9.

Brulet, Lysiane   'La Dentelle aux fuseaux dans le Queyras'. *OIDFA Bulletin*, vol. 8, no. 1, 1988.

Burkhard, Claire   *Fascinating Bobbin Lace*. Haupt, 1986.

Bussagli, Mario (ed.)   *Cotton and Silk Making in Manchu China*. Rizzoli, 1980.

Campbell, R.H. (ed.)   *States of the Annual Progress of the Linen Manufacture, 1727-54*. Edin. HMSO, 1964.

Carter, H.R.   *The Spinning and Twisting of Long Vegetable Fibres*. Griffiths, 1904.
   'Rope, Twine and Thread making'. *Technical Handbook*, no. 3. Bale and Danielsson, London, 1909.

*CIBA Review*   no. 28. 'The Spinning Wheel', 1939.
         no. 33. 'Bark Fabrics', 1940.

*Collection of Political Tracts*   no. 30. 'Mr Francis Jenk's Speech in 1679'.

Cook, J. Gordon   *Handbook of Textile Fibres*. Merrow 1968.

Crawford, Morris de Camp   'Peruvian Fabrics'. *Anthrop. Papers Am. Mus. Nat. Hist*. Vol. XII, no. 4, 1916. pp. 105-191.
   *The Heritage of Cotton*. NY, 1924.

Crawford, W.H.   *The Irish Linen Industry*. Ulster Folk and Transport Museum and Irish Linen Guild, c1986.

Crowfoot, Grace M.   *Hand-spinning and Wool Combing*. Ruth Bean, 1974 reprint of 1931 ed.

Daremberg, Charles and Saglio, Edmund   *Dictionnaire des antiquités grecques*. 1877-1919.

Despierres, Mme G.   *Alençon Lace*. 1886 ed. translated by Roberta Morgan. Aberdeen Univ. Press, 1987.

Earnshaw, Pat.   *Bobbin and Needle Laces, Identification and Care*. Batsford 1983.

English, W.   'A Survey of the principal references to fashion fabrics in the diary of Samuel Pepys'. *Journal Text. Inst*, vol. 40, no. 3, March 1949.

Felkin, William   *History of Machine-wrought Hosiery and Lace Manufacture*. David and Charles, 1967 reprint of 1867 ed.

Garner, W.   *Textile Laboratory Manual*. vol. 5, *Fibres*. Heywood, 1967.

Hald, Margrethe   *Ancient Danish Textiles from Bogs and Burials*. Nat. Mus. Denmark, 1980.

Hall, A.J.   *The Standard Handbook of Textiles*. London, 1950.

Hall, Rosalind   *Egyptian Textiles*. Shire, 1986.

Henneberg, Alfred von   *The Art and Craft of Old Lace*. Batsford, 1931.

Heyn, A.N.J.   *Fibre Microscopy*. Intersc. Man. no. 2. NY, 1954.

*Identification of Textile Materials.* Text. Inst. Manch., 1985.

Jørgensen, Lise Bender  *Prehistoric Scandinavian Textiles.* Copenhagen, 1986.

Kent, Kate Peck  'The Cultivation and Weaving of Cotton in the Prehistoric Southwestern United States'. *Trans. American. Phil. Soc.* vol. 47, pt. 3, 1957.

Kirby, R.H.  *Vegetable Fibres.* Leonard Hill, London, 1963.

'Lace and Lacemaking'. *Chamber's Repository of Instructive and Amusing Tracts, c*1860.

Lee, C.H.  *A Cotton Enterprise, 1795-1840.* Manch. Univ. 1972.

Levey, Santina and Payne, Pat. *Le Pompe.* Ruth Bean, 1982.

'Making the finest Cotton Yarns for Laces'. *Lace and Emb. Review.* January-June, 1911. pp. 29-30.

Marsden, R.  *Cotton Spinning.* George Bell, 1884.

Matthews, J.M.  *Textile Fibres.* Chapman and Hall, 1924.

McIntyre, J.  *The Chemistry of Fibres.* Edward Arnold, 1971.

Mitchell, Lillias  *Irish Spinning, Dyeing and Weaving.* Dundalgan Press, Dundalk, 1978.

Newberry, Percy E.  *Archeological Survey of Egypt, Beni Hasan.* 1893-4.

Nordland, Odd  *Primitive Scandinavian Textiles in Knotless Netting.* Oslo Univ. Pres, 1961.

Oliver, Thomas  'The Relation between Normal Take-up or Contraction and Yarn Number for the same Degree of Twist in Twisted Threads', and other articles on twist. *Proc. Roy. Soc. Edin.* vol. 27, 1907 (pp. 93, 107, 244, 264).

Picken, M.B.  *Sewing Materials.* Women's Inst. London, 1925.

Pringle, A.V.  *The Theory of Flax Spinning.* Carter Pub., Belfast, 1949.

*The Mechanics of Flax Spinning.* Carter Pub., Belfast, 1951.

Ryder, M.L.  'Merino History in Old Wool'. *Textile History,* vol. 18, no. 2, Autumn 1987.

Sabbe, Ernest  *Historie de l'industrie Linière en Belgique.* Brussels, 1945.

Simon, M.E.  'Unification du Numérotage des Fils - La Soie - titrage et numérotage'. *Bulletin de la soc. d'Encouragement pour l'Industrie nationale.* Oct., 1903.

Smith, Betty and Block, Ira  *Textiles in Perspective.* Prentice-Hall, 1982.

Sonday, Milton  'Natural Forces and their Effect on Basic Lace Laws'. *Kant,* Proc. Textieldag 25, April 1985, pp. 61-73. Textielcommissie Musea, Amsterdam, 1987.

*Textile Terms and Definitions.* Text. Inst. Manch., 1975.

*The Textile Educator.* Huddersfield, 1889. pp. 621-3, 642-4.

Thomas, S.F.  *Etudes sur les Tulles et Dentelles.* Paris, 1886.

*Timeless Textiles.* West Surrey College of Art and Design Ex. 1986.

Trecco, G.B.  *Coltivazione e Governo del Lino Marzuolo.* Vicenza, 1792.

Vale, Edmund  *The World of Cotton.* Rbt Hale, 1951.

Wakefield, Sam  *Cotton doubling and twisting.* 1916.

Welters, Dr Linda  'Embroidery on Greek Women's Chemises'. *Needle and Bobbin Club Bull.* vol. 67, 1984.

*Willimantic at the Centennial Exhibition, 1876.*

Wily, John  *A Treatise on the Propagation of Sheep, the Manufacture of Wool, and the Cultivation and Manufacture of Flax.* Williamsburg, 1765.

Wykes, A.L.  *The Working of Viscose Silk.* Heywood, n.d.